Pumpkin, Pumpkin:

Folklore, History, Planting Care, and Good Eating

Anne Copeland

All rights reserved. No part of this book may be transmitted in any form or by any means, electronic or mechanical, including photocopying, recording, or by any information storage and retrieval system without written permission from the author, except for the inclusion of brief quotations in a review.

The author of this book has written it in good faith that anyone using the book knows how to cook and uses basic sense in creating the recipes. It is the sole responsibility of the persons using this book to do so wisely.

Copyright ©1986 by Anne Copeland MacCallum
Copyright ©2009 by Anne Copeland
Copyright©2019 by Anne Copeland
Created in the United States of America
Copeland, Anne, 1941 -

Pumpkin, Pumpkin:
Lore, History, Nutrition, Planting Care,
    and Good Eating
1. Cookbook - Pumpkins
2. Pumpkins - Nutrition and Planting Care
3. Pumpkins - History and folklore

First Ed. – Anne Copeland MacCallum, San Pedro, CA, 1986
Second Ed. - Anne Copeland, Lomita, CA 2009
Third Ed. – Anne Copeland, Yucaipa, CA 2019

ISBN: 9781719980982
anneappraiser@gmail.com

Cover photo by Susanne Jutzeler from Pexels.

CONTENTS

INTRODUCTION 6
HISTORY OF THE PUMPKIN 8
FOLKLORE AND TRADITIONS 13
    Spooks & Lanterns 23
THE PUMPKIN AND ITS RELATIVES 26
GROWING YOUR PUMPKIN 27
    Varieties of Pumpkins 32
    Little Beasties that Go Chomp in the Night 47
    Hybridization 48
    Harvesting Fruits, Blossoms and Leaves 50
PUMPKINS FOR NUTRITION AND HEALTH 52
STORAGE AND PREPARATION 54
    Pre-drying Treatment 54
    Using a Dryer 55
    Sun Drying 55
    Using Dried Pumpkin 56
    Freezing 56
    Canning 57
    Hot Pack Method for Cubes 58
    Hot Pack Method for Strained Pumpkin 58

RECIPES 59

    Tummy Ticklers 62

    Soups & Salads 70

    Breads, Batters & Biscuits 97

    Main Events 121

    Asides 149

    Sauces 171

    Jams, Pickles, Drinks & Other Good Things 176

    Sweet Things 183

APPENDIX 239

RECIPE INDEX 242

ACKNOWLEDGMENTS

This book is dedicated with honor to Spencer Heath MacCallum who encouraged and supported me through the first publishing of this book and his good wife, Emi, who helped collate and comb bind the first edition; and to the surgeon who performed my knee replacement, allowing me to sit for hours with my knee up on another chair while I edited and redid the second edition. I want to specially thank Richard Dean McCoy, the love of my life, who unselfishly encouraged and supported this third edition rework and updating. I wish to also thank Barbara Williamson, who encouraged me through the last update of this book.

INTRODUCTION

Driving along a back road in Virginia one bright October day many years ago with a good friend, I suddenly said, "Pumpkins! We're coming to pumpkins!" My friend seemed confused because I really wasn't familiar with that part of Virginia at all. I had never been there before. But as we rounded a curve, there was a great field of large, golden pumpkins.

I guess I have always had a special affinity for pumpkins. Pumpkin season has always been more than a time to don masks, carve Jack o'Lanterns and put out treats for tricksters. It is a season that in my mind lasts long beyond the last pumpkin pie of Thanksgiving.

The season of the pumpkin is something is something of a paradox. At a time when many growing things are resting and bare, the pumpkin is at its peak of abundance under the autumn sun.

Each year, the selecting of the pumpkin has been one of my special adventures. The special hunt takes place through little out-of-the-way fruit and vegetable stands and sometimes in other nearby towns, until just the right pumpkin is discovered. And each year the characteristics of the just-right pumpkin change. One year it might be huge and fat, and the deepest orange possible, while the next year it might be tall and lean, and as pale as a new-rising moon. I never know until I see the just-right pumpkin what its characteristics will be.

The pumpkin is turned in my hands for the best viewing angle. I rub my hands over it, pushing the stem a little to be sure it is sturdy and fresh. The feel is important. A good pumpkin, I have determined over the years, must always have at least one slight flaw in its otherwise perfect complexion. This much I know each year, although what the flaw will be remains a mystery until I see it.

When the pumpkin arrives safely home, the first task is to find a special place where it will sit happily -- a place that is not too hot and sunny. It must be a place where little cat paws cannot accidentally cause it to somehow fall over and roll off onto the floor. For anyone who owns cats, I am sure you can identify with this phenomenon.

In the past, I delighted in giving the pumpkins special carved or painted faces, but in recent years I realized each pumpkin has its own face. The pumpkin's natural face is something like those old radio programs; it has a magical quality that is created out of the soul of each of us.

The demise of the pumpkin is never a sad occasion, for every part has eventually been made into something that I continued to enjoy. Sometimes I just save the seeds, and I dream that perhaps one of those seeds will turn into a special pumpkin. It is unlikely, however that I will ever know, for I have never owned a piece of land large enough to grow all the seeds from the pumpkins.

One year I made necklaces of the seeds, making holes through each one with a needle while they were wet and later removing the avrils (the filmy membranes covering the seeds), and stringing the seeds alternately with wood beads.

And so it has been that each year as my pumpkin season has come to an end, I have found myself seeking special recipes and other interesting information about these wonderful fruits. My quest to find these recipes has taken me through many an adventure, and I have made many friends along the way.

I am happy to share my joy of pumpkins with you here.

— Anne Copeland

HISTORY OF THE PUMPKIN

No one can say with certainty where the pumpkin was born, nor exactly when. Paleobotanists, working to piece together a coherent picture of agricultural development in the New World, have found pumpkin seeds dating back to 7,000 BC, preserved in dry caves in the Tamaulipas Mountains of northeastern Mexico, indicating that they were cultivated at that time. But the question remains, if that is the earliest sign that they were being cultivated, how many centuries earlier did some wandering soul first find courage enough, or hunger enough, to eat the bright orange globes?

There are early literary references to pumpkins too--or at least to some type of plant that loosely resembled pumpkins--from many parts of the world. We still have no idea what these early "pumpkins" might have looked like.

The Chinese may have grown some form of pumpkins in the sixth and seventh centuries, and Africa claims to have had one variety prior to the advent of European or American Contact. Even Pliny the ender, in first-century Rome, wrote of a large, trailing vine with a globular fruit, which has sometimes been translated as being a pumpkin. On the other side of the world, pre-Columbian Peruvians fashioned clay pottery in the unmistakable form of pumpkins, suggesting that the fruit played a predominant part in their culture.

In seventh century China, the Minister of Agriculture for Emperor Chung wrote a description of the pumpkins, squash and cucumbers that crept up the banks along roadways, ornamenting the landscape with their bright blossoms.[1] During the season of the Fifth Moon, the Chinese presented pumpkins as an offering to the deities, along with a variety of other fruits, vegetables, grains, meat and fish.[2]

Pumpkin cookery must have become some-thing of an art. A Chinese cook once recorded the follow-ing recipe: "Cut the (roughly translated) pumpkin into slices and let stand in the juice of golden limes. Beat to a sea-foam the whites of two eggs and make into a paste with the yellow of one rice flower and a drop of cinnamon. Dip each slice of pumpkin into the paste and fry in sesame oil to the color of gold. Sprinkle with powdered Lichee nuts and sugared ginger and eat while smoking hot."[3] Pumpkin blossoms were eaten as well as the flesh of the pumpkin; cooked with duck, the blossoms were considered a delicacy as they are to this day.

The pre-Columbian peoples of Mexico and Peru prized the seeds of the pumpkin as well. The seeds were prepared and eaten in a variety of ways. Sometimes the flesh of the mature pumpkins was discarded. Archae-ological evidence suggests that the earliest pumpkins were eaten when they were green and immature.[4]

Books of the ancient Maya recovered from Chichén Itzá, a once powerful religious center in the jungles of Yucatan, gave us an idea of the market value of pumpkins in Mexico before the Conquest. The Indians used cacao beans, highly prized for chocolate drinks and sweets, as currency. Pumpkins sold for four cacao beans, as compared with rabbits, which sold for ten, whereas human slaves could be purchased for one hundred.[5] It seems strange to think of a human being worth twenty-five pumpkins or one hundred cacao beans.

Uses of the pumpkin throughout the world have been

as varied as the people using them. In the days when corrugated- iron roofs were popular in South Africa, it was a common sight to see pumpkins stacked on top of the houses to provide stability. There they were kept for many months without deteriorating.[6]

The pumpkin is a food staple of South Africa, and a wealth of ceremonialism has grown up concerning the preparation and use of it. South Africans prepare the pumpkin in highly imaginative ways, utilizing even the leaves. Porridges, butters, soap and beers are but a few of the products.

It is believed that the French introduced the pumpkin, or *pompion*, into England, where it found favor on all social levels. The poor removed the seeds, stuffed the pumpkin with apples and sweet herbs, baked it over a hot fire, and ate it whole. This was perhaps the earliest form of pumpkin "pie." English folk of more substantial means sliced their pumpkins, fried them with apples, sweet herbs and spices and sometimes currants, then added sugar and beaten eggs and put the whole into lidded crusts called *coffins*. Both of these types of "pies" were baked for many hours, for the Europeans believed that uncooked fruits were dangerous. By the eighteenth century, the pumpkin had lost its popularity among folk of substantial means, but it continued to be favored by the commoners.[7]

For the American Indians, pumpkin, along with corns, beans and squash, was one of the "four sisters of agriculture. European travelers reported that the fields, which dotted the Indian landscape, always contained these four staples.[8]

Huron Indian women sprouted pumpkin and other seeds by gathering large quantities of rotted wood from old stumps in the forest. They powdered the rotted wood by pounding it, then placed it in a large box of bark. In this they planted more seeds than the number they would need, then suspended the box over the smoke of a fire, which warmed the damp wood powder slowly. Within a few days, the seeds sprouted. When the plants were of the right size, they were thinned out and planted in the field.[9]

The Indians ate their pumpkins baked whole in wood ashes, boiled, or sometimes made into a sort of succotash with corn and beans. Occasionally, pumpkin flesh was cooked with meat stews, or eaten when green and immature.[10] The seeds of the pumpkin were considered a delicacy and were roasted or eaten raw. The Indians also sliced the pumpkin into rings, which they hung up and dried. Later they ground the dried pumpkin into flour and blended it with cornmeal to make bread. Although liquor, as such, was unknown to the Indians prior to the coming of the Europeans, they did make a fermented drink from the pumpkin.[11]

To the colonists arriving in America, unprepared for their new environment, the "four sisters of agriculture" represented survival. The importance of the pumpkin for them is indicated by an old New England verse:

"For pottage, and puddings, and custards, and pies,
Our pumpkins and parsnips are common supplies.
We have pumpkins at morning, and pumpkins at noon;
If it were not for pumpkins, we should be undone."[12]

The pumpkin may never have seen as much use, or such a variety of ways of preparing it as in New England. Like their poor European cousins, the colonists made their pies of whole pumpkins, stuffing the cavities with spices, sugar and milk, and replacing the lids. The pumpkins were then baked in brick ovens in their own flesh. Stewed with cider, pumpkin made an excellent butter similar to apple butter in texture. Dried and ground into flour, it was often mixed with cornmeal for bread, as the Indians had done. The pumpkin was a hard-times substitute for other staples as well. Pumpkin syrup, for example, substituted for molasses, and during the Revolutionary War, Americans made pumpkin sugar. Even the cattle were fed pumpkins when other feed was in short supply. Finding the soil unsuitable for growing barley and hops, the men of the New England colonies made a brew using pumpkins, maple sugar and persimmons.

As America became settled and agricultural methods improved, the use of pumpkins diminished. Perhaps this was because they require so much space to grow. Although somewhat less widely used today, it is hardly an exaggeration to say that the early Americans grew up with pumpkins as a staple in their diets.

A little known fact of history is that at one time the Port of Boston was called Pumpkinshire, presumably because of the widespread popularity and use of the fruit there.[13]

FOLKLORE AND TRADITIONS

"Peter, Peter, Pumpkin Eater,
Had a wife and couldn't keep her.
He put her in a pumpkin Shell,
And there he kept her very well."

American pumpkin lore tends to be humorous and light, generally containing one or more of the following elements: the biggest, the fastest, and so on. Such lore creates an additional dimension in the everyday lives of the people.

In other world cultures, pumpkins often have important roles in the mythology. One East Indian myth tells of a man whose son became ill and died. The man put his son's body inside a pumpkin and carried it to the foot of a mountain. Much later, he returned to the area and opened the pumpkin. To his great surprise, a great deal of water, fish and even a few whales flowed out. When the people of the father's town heard the story, they rushed out to catch the fish, accidentally breaking the pumpkin into pieces. From each piece flowed a river. Some of the water became an ocean, covering the earth. Other myths from India tell of the pumpkin yielding a year's supply of rice, and of pumpkins, which provide treasures of silver and gold. One pumpkin provides a stream of oil.[1]

The pumpkins of India aren't always presented in such serious roles, however. There is a tale of a boiling pumpkin that the natives believe is talking. And a numbskull believes he is dead when a pumpkin falls on his head. Sometimes the people of India seem to be angry with the pumpkin, as in the tale about God being blamed for letting the pumpkin vines produce larger fruit than the nut trees.[2]

The Laotians, people from the upper part of Indo-China, believe that all the races of eastern Indo-China came from a pumpkin. A myth from the eastern hill people suggest that a pumpkin was a version of the Tree of Knowledge of Good and Evil as we know it in the Bible.[3]

Sometimes the pumpkin is given a voice, and becomes a strange creature. One African myth tells of an evil wizard-like man who was bitten by a snake and died. Some pumpkins sprang up on the spot where he died. Children passing the pumpkins wished to split them with their father's sword. At this point, one of the pumpkins became angry and began to pursue the children. The pumpkin talks to the villagers, inquiring where the children have gone. To the relief of all concerned, the villagers capture the pumpkin and burn it to ashes. This is not the type of story to read the children before sending them off to their beds.[4]

The Swahilis have a myth of a pumpkin, which springs up from a dead mother's grave, apparently a symbol of rebirth.[5]

A beautiful Chinese story tells of two families separated only by a wall. Each family planted pumpkins on their side of the wall, and when the plants reached the top of the wall, they joined together and became one plant.

After the plant flowered, it developed a huge fruit, which both families wanted to pick when it became ripe. The families discussed the situation for a long time before deciding that each should take a half. Upon cutting the gourd open, they found a beautiful little girl inside. The two families looked after the little girl and named her Meng Chiang.

When the girl grew up, she became the wife of a man who had come to China to help build the Great Wall. The evil emperor who had ordered the wall to be built soon heard of Meng Chiang's beauty and declared that he would make her the empress. Unable to resist the wicked emperor's request, she agreed that she would marry him after he met three conditions.

First there was to be a festival in honor of her husband, who had died of a broken heart. The emperor and all his officials were to be present at her husband's burial. And finally, the emperor was to build a terrace for Meng Chiang to make a sacrifice to her husband.

As soon as Meng Chiang's requests were completed, she climbed up the terrace, cursing the emperor for his wickedness, and jumping into the river below. The angry emperor ordered his men to cut her body into little pieces. When they did as they were ordered, the little pieces changed into little silver fish, in which the soul of the faithful girl lived forever.[6]

Chinese pumpkins have been known to give birth to stranger things than pretty little girls. One such pumpkin myth tells of a very powerful, but stupid man who wished to exchange goods to get the pumpkins belonging to some mountain women. He believed the pumpkins to be the eggs of an elephant.[7]

Early American pumpkin lore often has a richness of language. For this reason, I have chosen to present some of the best tales here just as I found them.

The following tale comes from the southern part of the United States, and was told by a black plantation worker a long time ago.

"Tol' Jack to get de fastes' horse in de lot. He got up on de horse to go out on de plantation to drop de pum'kin seed. He made a hole wi' de stick, dropped de seed. Horse ran as fas' as he could. Vine ran faster. You clim' up on top of that leaf an' holler. Dat pum'kin vine had pum'kins on it.

"My marster had two hawgs. Dey went away. De hawg feeder name Jack. "Jack, we got to look for dem hawgs. Won't do to let 'em run away. Go to house, ask mistress for half a shoulder of meat, an' cook me some bread." De hawgs had eat a hole in dat pum'kin, and' staid in dere until nex' plantin' time. From dat pum'kin vine they build a hotel in Richmon'. Made pretties' doors an' winders you ever saw."[8]

New England, where pumpkins played such an important part, is a treasure trove of pumpkin lore. The following incident is taken from the "Blue Laws," which Reverend Samuel A. Peters included in his *General History of Connecticut*. He claimed that the outlandish laws were created and enforced by the Puritans, but nearly all of them have since been discovered in the New Haven Statutes.

New Haven is celebrated for having given the name of "pumpkin-heads" to all New Englanders. It originated from the "Blue Laws," which enjoined every male to have his hair cut round by a cap. When caps were not to be had, they substituted the hard shell of a pumpkin, which being put on the head every Saturday, the hair is cut by the shell round the head. "Whatever religious virtue is supposed to be derived from the custom, I know not; but there is much prudence in it. First, it prevents the hair from snarling; secondly, it saves the use of combs, bags and ribbons; thirdly, the hair cannot incommode the eyes by falling over them; and fourthly, such persons as have lost their eyes for heresy and other wickedness, cannot conceal their misfortune and disgrace."[9]

Pigs and pumpkins seem to go together, at least in folktales, as we shall see from this tale from New England.

"Now I can't vouch for this story. T'was told to me way back when I was a little shaver. I won't say as to whether it was true or not because I wasn't there. It all happened long 'fore I was born. My Grandsir now, lived on a farm down on the little Ox Bow. There were nice fertile fields down along the river same as there are now. One fall, Grandsir turned his pigs out on the Ox Bow same as usual. There was one big old sow about ready to farrow. She got lost and didn't come up to eat with the others and you may know there is somethin' far wrong when a pig won't come to dinner.

"Well, sir, my Grandsir and a couple others long about dark went hunting that sow. They traveled all over the little Ox Bow. Finally they went down toward the bank of the river. It's forty -- fifty feet wide there. On the bank was a pumpkin vine, a goral mighty big one, leaves like umbrellas. Out from the vine was growin' stalks, big ones, and two of them stalks had grown together. You know, the way molasses candy looks when you pull it flat this way. Well, the old sow's tracks went right up to that vine and disappeared, just vanished into thin air. That vine stretched right out across the river. Clear over to the New Hampshire side.

"Warn't no other place the old sow could have gone, so Grandsir knew she must have crossed the river on that pumkin vine. Wait now, that warn't all of it. The men got a canoe and crossed the river. That was way before the bridges were built. They went along by it and there were the sow's tracks. Way back a bit they came across a big pumkin, the biggest one they ever saw. Around the other side was a little hole about so big. They peaked in and there was the old sow sleepin' sound with a whole litter of piglets cuddled up to her."10

Pumpkins often seem to travel fast and far. Here is a short tale about a pumpkin with quite a reputation.

"A traveler on a miserably lean looking steed was hailed by a Yankee who was hoeing his pumpkins by the fifteen dollars. So he paid him the fifteen dollars, was on his way home with the punkin. So he was on side of a hill and he stumbled and fell. Punkin went rolling down the roadside. "Hallo friend," said the farmer, "Where are you bound?" I am goin' to settle in the western country," replied the other. "Well, get off and straddle this here pumpkin vine -- it will grow and carry you faster than that there beast."[11]

If one is inclined to exaggerate, the pumpkin will provide wonderful subject matter. The following folktale takes place in Michigan, with two fellows arguing over the merits of their grandfathers' crops.

"They got to arguing about raising stuff. One of the boys said, 'My granddaddy is the best farmer around here. He raised a watermelon that weighed 500 pounds.'

"The second fellow said, 'P'shaw, that's nothing. Right out of town down there on the levee (that was in New Orleans), my granddaddy raised a punkin was so big they had forty men to pull the saw, they had a scaffold forty feet high, and the punkin was eight hundred rods long. And the saw was four hundred feet long. They saw cut it in half. Then they cut one of them halves into quarters. They prised it loose so they could get into the seeds. And the seeds was so big they was making ships out'n them. And they used the other half for the roundhouse for the I.C. (Illinois Central) in New Orleans.'"[12]

The following tale is another version of the pumpkin believed to be an egg. It is told by a black man in

Michigan. The foolish man in this case is an Irishman.

"This I'shman he went to town and he seed a punkin. He axed the man what was it. He said, 'Well, that's a mare's egg.' He axed him, well, what did he want for it. Told him hill. Up jumped a rabbit. I'shman said, 'Cup caller, cup caller, here's yo' mammy.' Thought it had hatched that quick, and rabbit just settling down there."[13]

The last tale is a favorite of mine. It has a little bit of everything and everyone in it. It is titled "*The Perambulatin' Pumpkin*."

"Down in Beaverdam Valley the mountain folk had gathered for the county fair. Mr. Zeke Calloway held up a bulging pumpkin decorated with the blue ribbon for the first prize, and grinned triumphantly at his neighbor and rival, Mr. Hank Huggins.

'Reckon you don't grow pumpkin like that on your side of the mountain!' he crowed.

'Law me,' drawled Hank, who had been known on occasion to stretch the truth somewhat. 'Law me, that little bitty thing would look like a peanut beside the pumpkins in my patch.'

'Mighty funny thing you didn't bring any of your monstrous pumpkins to the fair,' sniggled Zeke. '"Mighty funny.'

'Well, now, to tell you the truth, I was aiming to bring one, but we had a little accident up in our place this morning. It broke up my plans somewhat.'

'What kind of accident?' asked Zeke suspiciously.
'Well, you see, it was this way. My wife had laid off to bring a pumpkin pie to the fair. She was up early baking the crust, and as soon as it was done, she climbed up the mountain to the field where the pumpkins were a-growing among the cornstalks.

'Of course, all the pumpkins were too big and too heavy to carry, so she set out to cut a slab of one, enough to make the filling for her pie.

'Seems she had trouble with that, too. Those pum'kins were so thick though that her arm wasn't long enough to reach into the inside where the juicy part was. But she was bound to get some of the very best for she meant to take first prize with her pie. So what did she do but back out a big hole and climb through it right into the center of that pumpkin.

Now that would have been alright if the field where I planted 'em hadn't been so steep. But you know how it is -- sometimes a pumpkin will break off the vine by its own weight and go rolling down the mountain.

'Well, you can just picture what happened when that hefty wife of mine added her weight to the strain already on that vine. Before she knew what was happening, she was tumbling head over heels inside that pumpkin as it rolled out of the cornfield.

'I was in the barn lot hitching up the mule to the wagon when I looked up and saw it coming, a picking up speed every minute. Before I could gather my wits to think what to do, it had hit the lot fence with a crash that sent the rails flying like matches. It tore through the barnyard, hit my wagon amidships, and sent the wheels flying four ways at once. The chickens and ducks ran squawking for their lives.

'I could hear my old lady screeching and hollering, 'Oh, my pie! My pie!' as she went reeling on down the mountain inside that pumpkin.

'Well, sir, there wasn't a thing I could do about it, so I figured there wasn't any use to get excited. I went to the ledge and looked after it awhile as it went bumping and bounding down toward the valley, cutting a swath through the underbrush as it went.

'About halfway down I saw it bounce across the highway and crash into a covered wagon loaded with apples. Folks in the valley told me afterwards that apples rained down on 'em thick as hair for half an hour or so. They thought a miracle had happened up in the sky. Soon after that, I lost sight of the thing, so I went back to the barn.

"One look at my wagon told me I wasn't going to haul any pumpkins to the fair, but I didn't see any call to give up the trip. I could still go on mule back. The pumpkin had headed in that direction anyhow, and I thought I might as well jog down and see what had happened to my wife.

"Into the cabin I went and put on my store-bought Sunday clothes. As I was on my way out again, my eyes lit on a piecrust sitting on the kitchen table. It was nice and brown and crisp looking and it came to me that this must have been what my wife was a-screeching about as she went rolling down the mountain. I picked it up, wrapped it carefully so it wouldn't break, and put it into my saddlebag.

'Then I straddled my mule and ambled on down the trail, wondering a mite as I jogged along where my old lady could have ended up.

'When I got to Beaverdam, I began to get a suspicion that she had rolled right onto the fairground. There was a hole in the side of the fence that would have accommodated an elephant, and the trail of wreckage inside the grounds looked like a hurricane had torn through. Folks were running around like excited ants trying to fix up the damage.

'I followed the trail of ruin and at the end of it, sure enough, there sat my wife amidst the wreckage of the pumpkin. It had smashed against a stone chimney.

'Oh my pie, my pie! Now I've got no pie to take to the fair,' she was still a-wailing.

'Why honey, yes you have,' I said to her as I rode up. I put my hand into my saddlebag and brought out the piecrust.

"'But -- but, Hank,' she said. 'A pumpkin pie's got to have sugar and eggs and spices and I don't know what all.'

'Not this pumpkin, honey,' I said to her. 'The pumpkins I raise are flavored already. You just scoop out one of these pieces and spread it in the crust as is, and you'll have a finer, tastier pie than anybody at the fair.'

'Well, sir, she got up from there, brushed herself off a mite, straightened her hair a little, and fixed up that pie just as I told her to. You can see for yourself what the upshot was.

'Look over there now, across the table full of wild strawberry jam beside that fancy patchwork quilt hanging on the wall. There she stands. See that pie she's a-holding? That's the very pie and if it hasn't got a blue ribbon a-hanging to it, I'll eat my Sunday pants.

'Well, Hank,' said Mr. Zeke Calloway sourly, 'All I've got to say is, it's too bad they're not offering prizes for tall tales. If there were, there'd be two blue ribbons in your family.'"[14]

Spooks & Lanterns

What book about pumpkins would be complete without mentioning Halloween? I miss the holiday I knew as a child.

I remember parties with colorful trimmings of orange and black crepe paper hanging everywhere from the ceilings. Eyes that had been familiar seemed strange behind masks and sheets. What a shock it was to stick my face into the tub, trying to grab an apple with my teeth! The cold ran all the way to my toes. But I wouldn't give up until I got one. And pumpkin carving -- suddenly everyone became an artist. The tops came off, and hands dipped into the depths of the pumpkin to pull forth the membranes and seeds. There were popcorn balls, sticky and sickenly sweet, an important aspect of the night. The fragrance of hot apple cider filled my head and carried me off to a dream world. The fire danced over the logs, casting crazy patterns of light around the fireplace. The first hint of really cold weather could be felt in the air.

There were always stories of haunted houses. Every neighborhood must have had one. And then there was always someone who had gone to it -- *once*. I sat on the edge of the sofa, or curled up on the floor, hanging on every word.

For all my enjoyment of Halloween as a child, it wasn't until much later that I learned what the night's celebration was all about.

The word, "Halloween" means "holy or hallowed evening." It always comes on the day before All Hallows, or All Saints' Day, which comes on the first day of

November. The night might best be compared to a very short Mardi Gras. It is a time when people can "let their hair down" in preparation for the more solemn aspects of the holy day.

All Saints' Day was celebrated probably first in the seventh or eighth century at St. Peter's in Rome. A chapel was dedicated at that time for the purpose of honoring all the known and unknown saints.[1]

But the rites, which occurred on the preceding evening, actually stemmed from an earlier pagan festival. The Druids, members of a religious order among the Celts, occupied the land we now know as France and the British Isles. The Druid priests observed two important feasts -- *Beltane*, on the first day of May, and the autumn festival of *Samhain*, on the last day of October. Samhain, which occurred after the harvests had been gathered, marked the end of summer and the beginning of winter. Since the New Year of the Celts began on November 1, Samhain was something akin to our New Year's Eve.

At the beginning of the festivities that took place on Samhain, great bonfires were lit on the hilltops for the purpose of honoring the sun god and to frighten away any evil spirits that might be loose on that night.

It was some time before the American colonists as a whole began to take notice of the customs brought by the Gaelic immigrants, customs such as harvest feasts and the building of bonfires. Masks and lanterns have long been associated with Halloween, the masks vividly portraying the evil spirits and demons abound on that evening (reminiscent of the gargoyles and demons seated on the outside of Gothic cathedrals), and the lanterns that perhaps served as small, contained bonfires for portable, personal protection.

One tradition of lanterns says that the jack-o'-lantern harks back to an Irishman named Jack, who loved to play pranks on the Devil. Jack was punished by having to wander all over the world, neither in heaven nor hell, carrying a lantern to show him his way.[2]

It remains a mystery who first recognized the potential of the great orange pumpkins for combining the two ideas of mask and lantern. The lighting of the pumpkin lantern carved with grotesque faces may have been a way of symbolically burning the spirits away."

THE PUMPKIN AND ITS RELATIVES

The pumpkin is a member of a puzzling family, which is difficult to classify botanically. I enjoy thinking of it as the platypus of the vegetable set. While most people think of the pumpkin as a vegetable, botanists classify it as a fruit. And there is still some controversy among botanists as to whether pumpkins and squashes represent different plant types.

The pumpkin is not an ordinary fruit. It is a berry, difficult as that is to imagine. It is classified as a berry because it is a simple fruit, formed from a single pistil of the flower, and because it has no stones or papery cores. Grapes, tomatoes and blueberries are typical berries; they are fleshy throughout, and their outer layer, or exocarp, is a thin skin. The pumpkin is not a typical berry because of its hard rind. Along with its controversial cousins, the squashes, and its second cousins, the melons and cucumbers, the pumpkin is a kind of berry known as a *pepo*.[1]

Even the name 'pumpkin' is incongruous. The name is derived from the Greek *pepon*, meaning "cooked in the sun." The French corrupted the word to *poumpon*, and the English then corrupted it to *poumpion*, or *pompion*. Later it was given the suffix, '*kin*,' which always means the diminutive form of something. Perhaps the word was coined in jest, making fun of the fact that the pumpkin is so large, in the same way that a fat, clumsy man was sometimes called a '*bumpkin*.'[2]

GROWING YOUR PUMPKIN

Some people unceremoniously poke their pumpkin seeds into the ground, sometimes without even preparing the soil ahead of time. Despite such treatment, not because of it, pumpkins will sometimes begin to grow. In fact, they might even turn into rather nice pumpkins. But in my mind at least, growing them in such an unceremonious manner does not seem fitting for such a grand fruit. Like the Japanese tea ceremony, pumpkins have a mystique about them, which should involve their beginnings as well as their endings.

Before you spend hours browsing through the seed catalogs to determine which type of pumpkin to grow, it would be a good idea to take stock of your gardening area. If you have determined that you are going to grow any of the giants, you will need a lot of space; the vines can grow thirty to forty feet long for one plant! An area about four feet wide and thirty-five feet long will be about the right size. You can, of course, choose to grow the bush pumpkins, in which case you won't need much space. Or you can try training the longer pumpkin vines up a ladder, brick wall, trellis or pyramid planter. Simply tie the vines up as they grow, and suspend the pumpkins in slings. Growing them in this way can provide a real challenge.

If your pumpkins aren't going to be the focal point in your garden, you can put them off to one side, or at one end of your straight rows. You might choose to create a work of art in the garden, perhaps growing the pumpkins in a large circle surrounding other vegetables chosen for color and form. This will not be too difficult to do if you train your vines around the circle. Just be sure to leave pathways along the inside areas for maintenance and harvesting. You can create a Mandala effect of the bright colors. An attractive combination would be to have pumpkins on the outer circle, Swiss Chard and cauliflower alternately placed in the next circle, followed by red and green peppers, a circle of purple-pod beans and a center of Calico Indian corn or Squaw corn. Sketch out other forms of your preference on paper and plan what vegetables you might want to use, keeping in mind the growing habits and space requirements of each. A labyrinth of pumpkin vines would also be an interesting choice.

Once you have decided what to plant, you will need to prepare your soil. Almost every soil needs a little help before planting time. You can begin by digging trenches 18 to 24 inches deep. Get enough manure to make several layers in your gardening area. If you use chicken manure instead, it should be at least four months old so it will not burn your young plants. Many nurseries sell chicken manure.

Shovel in a layer of the manure, the compost, bone meal and lime, followed by a layer of soil. Continue this process, tamping the soil down as you work to avoid air pockets. You should finish with a layer of topsoil about six inches deep.

Make some depressions in the soil about three to four feet apart where you are going to plant your pumpkins. These will hold the water for the growing plants.

When your seeds arrive, you will be ready to plant them outdoors as soon as the danger of frost is past. Plant five to six seeds per "hill." A hill is nothing more than a group of seedlings that germinate, not a mound area.

When the seeds germinate, select the best two or three seedlings, pulling out the rest. Hard as it may be for you to do this, you will be thankful you thinned them later on.[1]

"Hot caps" will protect your pumpkin plants if a frost threatens. You can purchase them from one of the seed companies, or you can make them from newspaper, plastic, or milk cartons turned upside down. Avoid having the hot caps touch the seedlings. Leave plenty of air space, and be sure to remove them when the sun comes out and the frost danger is past.

If you live in an area where the frosts are likely to come late in the spring, or if you simply get anxious to start growing your pumpkins, you can start them indoors. One thing to remember about pumpkin seedlings is that they have lots of tiny roots, so they must be transplanted in a way that will avoid disturbing the root system. You can use peat pots, which can be planted, or you can make your own starter containers out of milk cartons. Cut the tops off and fill with a mixture of soil and manure. Plant two or three seeds in the center of each carton. When the seedlings come up, remove the smaller ones gently, leaving one plant in each carton. Carefully put three-fourths to one cup of water around the soil, then cover the top of the container with plastic wrap or waxed paper held in place with a rubber band, string or tape.[2]

Set the containers where they will receive at least a 70 degree temperature constantly. If the temperature gets above 80 degrees, the seeds will germinate too fast, becoming tall and leggy. The seeds do not need direct light to germinate, but once they do germinate, you will need to remove the covers and set the seedlings where they will receive at least four hours of direct sunlight (five to six hours is better). It will probably take about seven to twelve days for them to germinate, but if they are stubborn, it could take as long as eighteen days, so don't give up in despair if you don't see something green before that time.[3]

Water your seedlings every other day, taking care that the soil is damp, but not wet. Poke some small holes near the bottom of the milk cartons for drainage. Set your plants outdoors about four weeks after germination to get them used to the outdoor environment. Take care to protect them if the weather turns cold. After a few days or a week, you can set them in the ground. Cut the milk containers carefully away from the soil and life out the seedling and root ball in one piece. Plant it deep enough to cover the milk carton soil, allowing three-fourths to one inch extra soil for support. Tamp the soil down firmly and water deeply with a bubblier or hand-held hose.[4]

Water deeply once a week, preferably in the morning. Be careful not to sprinkle the leaves or you might have a mildew problem.
Fertilize your plants weekly or bi-weekly with a mild infusion of fish fertilizer or an infusion of manure (one part manure to three parts water).

Growing a really large pumpkin is actually not difficult. Simply begin the pumpkin growing in the normal way, and when the fruits begin to form, select the most promising one and pick the others off. One pumpkin per vine is the rule. You can also promote your pumpkin's growth by pinching off the vining tips.

To help the giant maintain a nice shape, burrow out a large depression for it and fill this with straw or some mulching material to provide a nice bed. Remember that you are not going to be able to turn it over readily when it begins to get really big. Besides, you shouldn't disturb your growing pumpkins any more than necessary as they might prematurely break from their stems.

If you live in an area where your weather gets cold in the fall, you should harvest your pumpkins before the first severe frost. The skin should be hard, and you should not be able to puncture it with fingernails. Leave at least an inch or more of your stem on the pumpkin, and cure it in the sun for seven to ten days. Do not wash your pumpkin before storing, but you can certainly wipe it clean if it is too dirty, using a very slightly damp paper towel. If you do this before you cure it, your pumpkin will be fine.

Varieties of Pumpkins

There are many interesting types of pumpkins out now for you to try. This descriptive list will help you select the right type of pumpkin for your garden space and particular use. This list was created after reviewing the many, many sources of seeds out there. Because resources for purchasing seeds seem to change so rapidly, I will not list them here. Even the varieties might change as they have from when this book was first published till now.

Giant Pumpkins

All of these pumpkins require very large garden spaces, but they all have the capability of becoming prize pumpkins. There are many more than listed here, but the number changes constantly and half the fun is discovering the new varieties.

Amish Pie

This excellent orange pumpkin can weigh up to 75 pounds. The flesh is sweet and moist. It is perfect for pies.

Big Moon

This is another orange pumpkin that can reach 40 - 200 pounds with a great display.

Big Max

This orange pumpkin is great for carving or as a novelty display. It can grow to 100 pounds.

Big Moose

These pumpkins are bright orange with slight ribbing. Depending on your growing methods, the fruit can weigh 50-125 plus pounds.

Dill's Atlantic Giant

This is the all-time giant, with weights from 100 - 900 pounds. It is a definite prizewinner.

Full Moon

Depending on weather and growing conditions, this giant white pumpkin can reach 60 - 90 pounds. The skin is fairly smooth with slight suturing and its white color is retained best when it's harvested at maturity. If left in the field too long after maturity, the skin color will turn to a creamy beige.

Prizewinner

This orange pumpkin can easily reach 75 - 150 pounds. It is an excellent display pumpkin, the kind you see at country fairs.

Wyatt's Wonder

This round, smooth, buttery-orange heirloom pumpkin can weigh from 70-100 pounds when mature.

Large Pumpkins

Aladdin (Harris Exclusive)

This 25-35 pound powdery mildew tolerant, semi-dark orange pumpkin has moderate ribbing and grows on vigorous semi-full vines.

Appalachian

This hybrid semi-bush has a dark orange pumpkin that weighs up to 25 pounds.

Aspen

This early semi-bush hybrid heirloom pumpkin grows between 18 - 20 pounds.

A&C Hybrid #300

This dark orange Semi-Bush is an early, nearly full bush that is smooth and grows 16 - 20 pounds.

A&C Hybrid #500

This bright orange vine has an 18 - 22 pound medium sized round pumpkin with medium deep ribs. It is excellent for carving, strong handles.

A&C Hybrid #510

This deep orange pumpkin has deep ribs and is very attractive and great for carving. It can grow to 22 - 26 pounds.

Big Autumn

This orange pumpkin is a big brother to Autumn Gold and can reach 15 - 20 pounds.

Howden Biggie

This deep orange pumpkin grows to 35 - 60 pounds. It was formerly called Howden's Field.

Early Autumn

This medium deep orange vining pumpkin can grow to 10 - 14 pounds.

Gold Strike - (More recent variety of "Rupp")

This dark orange vining hybrid pumpkin has dark colored ribbing similar to Howden. It can grow to 15 - 20 pounds.

Mother Lode

This orange Rupp hybrid semi-bush has superior uniformity and yield. It can reach 18 - 25 pounds.

Connecticut Field (Big Tom)

This Native American heirloom pumpkin has a history predating 1700. Its orange 20 - 25 pound fruit is good for canning, carving or stock feed.

Gold Rush

This deep orange vining pumpkin can reach 20 - 35 pounds. It is a Rupp Exclusive.

Half Moon

This very thick fleshed, mostly tall pumpkin can range from 14 - 16 pounds.

Howden (Harris Moran)

This dark orange vining pumpkin reaches about 20 pounds and is the leader in commercial production of Jack-O-Lantern pumpkins.

Jumpin' Jack

This Rupp exclusive pumpkin with medium dark gold color tends to be taller than wide and reaches 20 - 40 pounds.

Mammoth Gold

This medium orange vining irregularly shaped pumpkin is slightly ribbed and flattened where it rests on the ground. It grows to 20 - 40 pounds.

Super Herc

These dark orange, medium ribbed, full-sized vining and powdery mildew-resistant pumpkins reach 30 - 40 pounds.

Thomas Halloween

This 15 - 30 pound deep orange medium large pumpkin is a good choice for local markets or shipping.

Mid-Size Pumpkins

Wolf

This deep orange pumpkin with moderate ribbing, has the largest handles bar none. It can reach 15-25 pounds depending on your growing circumstances.

Autumn Gold

This pumpkin turns orange early in the growing season and runs around 10 pounds. It is an All-American Selections (AAS) Winner.

Cheyenne Bush

This orange pumpkin reaches seven pounds and grows on bush vines. It is a good choice if you have a shorter growing season or limited growing space.

Frosty

This orange semi-bush hybrid is an excellent bush Jack O'Lantern type that can grow to 10 pounds.

Funny Face

This orange semi-bush produces a runner after the fruit sets. It can reach 10 - 12 pounds.

Gladiator

This vigorous, semi-vine, powdery mildew resistant, deep orange, moderately ribbed pumpkin produce grows to 20-25 pounds. It is very uniform for size and shape.

Ghost Rider

A superior dark pumpkin that grows 10 - 12 pounds.

Jack Of All Trades

This dark orange smooth hybrid with sutures can grow to 10 - 12 pounds.

Jack O'Lantern

This orange pumpkin is uniformly round, smooth skinned, yellow thick flesh. It can reach 10 pounds.

Jackpot

These orange medium size pumpkins are good for pies and Jack-O'-Lanterns with highly productive vines. They can reach 10 - 18 pounds.

Harvest Moon

This is a good orange space saving semi-bush that grows to 10 - 18 pound.

Magic Lantern (Harris Exclusive)

This dark orange pumpkin with medium ribs produces 16 - 24 pound pumpkins on semi-vines. It is the #1 powdery mildew tolerant hybrid.

Magician

Magician is the first pumpkin variety to combine both powdery mildew tolerance and zucchini yellows mosaic virus tolerance into the same variety. The semi-vining, deep orange pumpkins with moderate ribbing can reach 10-16 pounds.

Merlin (Harris Exclusive)

This quality powdery mildew tolerant hybrid with uniformity in color and shape has a classic, slightly upright shape and a deep orange. It can reach 15-25 pounds.

Spirit

This 10 - 12 pound orange pumpkin grows on a semi-bush and is an AAS Winner that is good for pies or carving.

Sorcerer

This deep orange pumpkin with large handles and heavy ribbing was the 2002 All America Selections winner. It can reach 15-25 pounds.

Trick or Treat

This orange semi-bush 10 - 12 pound pumpkin is a good carver and good for pie. The entire seed is edible and easily crushed to extract the prized edible oil.

Wizard

This 10 - 14 pound pumpkin has a dark color with smooth textured skin with light rib, good yield.

Yellow of Paris

This French yellow pumpkin can weigh up to 25 pounds and is good for pies or other cooking.

Young's Beauty

This older, hard skinned, dark orange pumpkin reaches 8 - 10 pounds.

Pie Pumpkins

Baby Pam

This orange pumpkin is uniform in shape and color, has high yields, and runs around two pounds. It is excellent for pies.

Casper

The bluish-white skin of this 10 - 20 pound pumpkin gives it a spooky appearance. The flesh has a fine flavor makes good pies.

Cornfield

Farmers found this heirloom 10 - 15 pound pumpkin a good choice to grow between their corn crops. It is still a great choice for pies or jack-o-lanterns.

Jackpot (Harris Exclusive)

Jackpot was the first hybrid pumpkin. The bright orange-yellow pumpkin can reach 12-20 pounds, and it is a good pie pumpkin. The vines are only 2/3 the size of standard pumpkins so you get heavier production in less space.

Mystic Plus (Harris Exclusive)

This powdery mildew tolerant, deep orange, semi-vining pie pumpkin can grow to seven - eight lbs.

New England Pie

With its five to eight pound weight, this bright orange pumpkin makes good mini jack-o-lanterns, while the flesh has excellent flavor.

Peek a Boo

This medium dark pumpkin grows to three - four pounds, is uniform in size and shape and great for decorating.

Small Sugar (Asgrow Strain)

This orange five - six pound pumpkin has a distinctly superior handle (stem) when compared to other Small Sugar strains. It is a popular garden variety for pies or canning.

Spookie

This orange five - six pound pumpkin is a Sugar Pie-Jack O'Lantern cross and is uniform in shape and color.

Spooktacular

This orange vining hybrid addition from PETO can reach three - five pounds and is uniform in shape and color.

Sugar Treat

This deep orange, smooth ribbed semi-bush Rupp exclusive Baby Pam hybrid pumpkin grows to three pounds. Super handle and excellent color fruit.

Trickster

This deep orange semi-bush pumpkin is Ideal for decorations, reaches two - three pounds and gives high yields.

Triple Treat

This deep orange hulless seeded pie pumpkin from Burpee grows to four - six pounds.

Winter Luxury Pie

This heirloom pumpkin was introduced in 1893, improved and popularized by Gill Brothers Seeds by 1917. It is deep orange with a slightly netted surface and sweet tender flesh. It averages 6 1/2 pounds.

Miniature & Specialty Pumpkins

Apprentice

Apprentice is a smaller version of the popular Lil' Ironsides. Compact bush plants produce disease resistant, hard-shelled, burnt orange pumpkins with no ribbing that grow to one pound. They are good decorating and painting as they have a very long shelf life.

Baby Bear

This orange heirloom vining pumpkin is an All-America Selections Winner for 1993. It weighs up to two pounds and is disease resistant.

Baby Boo

This white one to four pound pumpkin should be planted later than Jack-B-Quick types because it will turn a pale yellow at full maturity. The hulless seeds can be baked or eaten raw; their taste resembles cashew nuts.

Buckskin

This hybrid pumpkin reaches up to 12 pounds and looks like a large buff colored acorn. It is good for processing.

Bumpkin

This space-saving semi-bush, bright orange pumpkin is tolerant to powdery mildew and grows up to one pound. It is good for displays.

Cannonball

This powdery mildew-resistant, burnished orange pumpkin grows on vigorous bushes and can reach five pounds.

Casper

This bright white vining smooth skinned pumpkin is a pretty addition to an ornamental garden.

Fairytale

This French heirloom orange pumpkin has a unique color, shape, flavor and baking quality that will be a good addition if you are doing fresh market sales. It grows up to 15 pounds.

Hokkaido

There are two varieties of Hokkaido pumpkins. One has a deep orange color and the other has a light green skin and both have yellow flesh. Hokkaido pumpkins have a tough outer skin and are very sweet inside. In Thailand, the line between certain type of squashes and pumpkins is blurred. Hard skinned pumpkins and squashes with yellow flesh are all called *Fug Tong*. Hokkaido pumpkins are available at most Oriental markets. They reach about eight pounds.

Hooligan

This unique multi-colored, deeply ridged ornamental pumpkin has a similar color pattern to Lil' Pump-Ke-Mon but the fruit are smaller in size (approximately 2" H x 3-4" W). This is a great autumn indoor or outdoor display pumpkin.

Iron Man

This powdery mildew tolerant and disease-resistant, hard shelled, dark orange pumpkin can grow to three - four pounds and it is great for painting.

Jack-B-Little

The smallest of the miniature pumpkins; charming and very rewarding to grow. Vines are covered with numerous pumpkins no more than 3" in diameter. They grow to one pound and are great for decoration.

Jack-B-Quick

This pumpkin has more ribs than the Jack-B-Little pumpkin with smaller, taller and darker orange fruit.

Jarrahdale

This superb pumpkin is from Jarrahdale in New Zealand. It has a very ornamental hard silvery skin with orange-yellow sweet, dry stringless flesh, that is excellent for eating, or in pies. It can grow to around nine pounds.

Lil' Ironsides (Harris Exclusive)

Although this dark orange, disease resistant pumpkin is a true pumpkin it has a tough hard shell much like an ornamental gourd and is not carveable. It is uniform in shape and can reach up to two pounds. Its shelf life takes it well into the spring and it has a hard, smooth shell, great for painting.

Long Island Cheese

Grown by many generations of farmers and gardeners in the New York area, this pumpkin has the size, shape, and appearance of a wheel of cheese. The buff colored pumpkins are six - ten lbs., and make great displays in the fall.

Lil' Pump-Ke-Mon (Harris Exclusive)

This white mini-pumpkin with orange and green stripes has a distinctive flattened shape with slight to medium ribbing emphasized by the stripes. It reaches one-two pounds.

Lumina

This white vining, 10 - 15 pound pumpkin is excellent for carving, painting or eating. When cut, the pumpkin has bright orange flesh.

Munchkin

This light orange miniature one - four pound pumpkin is well suited for arrangements and fall decorations.

Neon

This vivid, almost florescent orange pumpkin matures quicker than any other pumpkin variety. It is uniform in shape and can reach seven - eight lb.

Oz

This bright orange four - five pound pumpkin with yellow fruit and a smooth skin will reach its color early.

Red and blue Kuris

These pumpkins originated in Japan. The Red Kuri is a red-orange, ridged, pear-shaped pumpkin while the Blue Kuri is a smooth, slate blue-green, pear-shaped type. They have a sweet yellow flesh, grow to about 10 pounds, and are best for pies.

Cinderella

This unique pumpkin from France is reddish orange, and has a flattened, deeply ridged fruit. It offers surprising beauty, great yield and flavor. It will grow to 20 pounds.

Seminole

Cultivated in Florida by the Seminole Indians in the 1500's, this heirloom pumpkin keeps up to one year at room temperature. Large vines bear bell-shaped buff colored pumpkins with firm, deep orange flesh. The pumpkin weighs around 10 pounds and is resistant to vine borers. It is a good choice for hot, humid, disease-prone areas. Give it ample moisture and room to roam.

Snackjack

These 1 - 2-1/2 pound, medium-orange bush vine pumpkins with shallow ribs mature fast and produce hull-less seeds that can be roasted as a delicious snack.

Tennessee Sweet Potato Pumpkin (C. moschata)

These pear-shaped, creamy, white-skinned, faint green striped, 10 - 20 pound pumpkins do not look like what we would consider a "pumpkin." If stored properly they can last more than six months and make an excellent pie. In 1847 the variety was listed by New York seedsman Grant Thorburn as 'Green Striped Bell' and re-named by W. Atlee Burpee (Burpee Seeds) in 1883 to 'Tennessee Sweet Potato'.

Valenciano

Valenciano is a very pretty, ivory white pumpkin that will add color and interest to fall displays. The flattened pumpkins have orange flesh that may be used for cooking. They reach about 10 pounds.

There are many new pumpkins being introduced, so if this list isn't complete, it is because something new has come out since the book was begun. Half the fun is finding the new varieties and trying to grow them.

Little Beasties that Go Chomp in the Night

Depending on the area where you live, there might be a few hurdles to get over before you can count yourself among the successful pumpkin growers. You could wake up one morning and go out to check on your patch, only to find a very fat mole standing outside a rather large hole in your favorite pumpkin. Should such an event occur, I suspect you wouldn't appreciate the humor of it. If there are hungry moles, gophers or other little critters that pose a threat to your pumpkins, you might set some traps out -- hopefully a humane type. Or you might consider getting a kitty that goes outdoors.

When I wrote the first edition of this book, the pests were limited in number, but today, for whatever reason, there are many more pests and diseases to which the pumpkins, big and small, are mostly susceptible. In the first edition, I gave some solutions to some pests and diseases with which I was familiar, but now I believe the best thing I can do is to direct you to search the web sites for learning about how to deal with your pumpkin's pests and diseases. If you do not feel comfortable with that, the Department of Agriculture will have many good suggestions for your area, and also your local university botany depart-ment may have some good suggestions as well.

There are also many Internet sites that provide more information for you on whatever type of pumpkins you would like to grow.

Hybridization

You have been reading about the pumpkin and its relatives, the cucumbers, squash and melons, and now you are wondering whether to try for a melokin, a pumkumber or perhaps a squashkin. Well, forget about that. It won't work. I know they are relatives, and I know that we get some pretty strange crossbreeds in nature. For reasons which I do not thoroughly understand and which I am not going to attempt to explain, we cannot cross melons with squashes, pumpkins with cucumbers, or any other such combinations, with one exception.

Pumpkins can be crossed with some of the winter squashes. And of course, various pumpkin types, including the Japanese pumpkins, can be crossed. You might decide to try this and experiment to see what you get. You might also write to the various seed companies listed in the back of this book. They are very helpful, and new plant varieties are their business. Your local agricultural agent may also be of some help. I favor the experimental method, crude as it sometimes can be.

When you are crossbreeding pumpkins (or attempting to do so), you must hand pollinate them. Simply take a soft paintbrush or Q-tip and brush lightly around the inside of each flower. Without shaking or cleaning the brush, continue to brush the flowers of one plant and then the plant you want to cross with it. You must take care to do this in the summertime, since the flowers that form on the plant in the spring will not make pumpkins. You must wait until midsummer to get male and female flowers, at which time both types will grow on each plant.

If the pumpkins you end up with seem really unusual, you might want to contact the seed companies. Some are interested in purchasing seeds of "weird" plants. Even if they do not purchase your seeds, they can give you some good ideas about keeping the seeds for replanting.

Harvesting Fruits, Blossoms and Leaves

If you have a rather small garden, harvesting will not be a big job. The chances are that you will not have too many pumpkins ripening at the same time. Even so, harvesting your pumpkins can be an occasion to celebrate with your friends. If your pumpkin patch is large, you can have your friends and neighbors help you gather them in, celebrating afterward with a harvest dinner or party.

You should cut your pumpkins about a week before you take them in, to allow time for them to harden their skins and mature properly. You can tell if the pumpkin is ready to be cut by thumping it. It is ready when it has a good hollow sound. Be sure to bring the pumpkin in if there is to be a frost, however. Take care not to bruise them when moving them, although they are not as delicate as some other fruits and vegetables.

Unless you think that any you have stored away might spoil if they are not used up right away, it is generally best to use freshly gathered pumpkins for canning or freezing.

When you are picking pumpkin blossoms for use, pick them early in the morning. That is the time when they will be open and can readily be rinsed. You can keep them well until you need them later in the day by floating them in ice water in the refrigerator. The blossoms can be picked through mid-summer. After that, if you want pumpkins, you must stop picking the blossoms.

Pumpkin leaves can be used for cooking also. Take care not to take too many if you want pumpkins as the vine will not be able to produce enough chlorophyll to nourish the pumpkins properly. You might consider growing some pumpkin plants strictly for their leaves and blossoms.

If you are growing a giant pumpkin, it can present you with some harvesting problems. You will need to enlist the help of your neighbors, perhaps scooting the pumpkin onto a heavy rug or blanket to protect it during the move.

PUMPKINS FOR NUTRITION AND HEALTH

A versatile foodstuff, the pumpkin offers other benefits as well. The seeds and flesh are thought to have medicinal value. From a description of New Spain written in 1774 comes the following: "The pepita (pumpkin seed) has a fruit like a hazelnut. Two or three in the morning are said to be good for the stomach -- but if swallowed in some quantity will lead to a painless death."[1] I suspect the last part is an unqualified statement. Pumpkin seeds are also said to be beneficial for ridding the body of internal parasites. And the Anatolian Turks, the Hungarian gypsies and the mountain dwelling Bulgarians knew that the pumpkin seeds preserved the prostate gland and thus male potency They are valuable for building up the male hormone as well.[2] Pumpkin seeds have long been used as a diuretic. A tea recipe for that purpose, and which is also said to improve blood sugar tolerance, is included in the recipe section.

In addition to these medicinal benefits, pumpkin seeds are highly nutritious. Pumpkin seeds are a very good source of the minerals phosphorous, magnesium and manganese. They are also a good source of other minerals including zinc, iron and copper. In addition, pumpkin seeds are a good source of protein and vitamin K (17.73 mcg). They are a good fiber source (1.35 g) and vitamin A (13.10 IU). They have 0% cholesterol and provide a good amount of protein (8.47 g).[3]

The Mayan Indians used sap made from pumpkin flesh as a remedy for burns. The flesh of pumpkin is said to be helpful for cases of dropsy, inflamed or infectious intestines, ulcers and hemorrhoids, and in raising the blood pressure for those with low blood pressure.[4]

Good sources of information on pumpkin nutritional values can be found at The World's Healthiest Foods, www.whfoods.org.

STORAGE AND PREPARATION

Aside from telling you the various ways to prepare the pumpkin and use it, I am going to assume that you, the readers, are intelligent enough to know that I when I write "one pound pumpkin, cubed," it means that you separate the flesh from the skin, remove seeds and membranes, and cut the flesh into nice cubes.

Generally speaking, if you are growing pumpkins, you will certainly have more than you can eat at one sitting. Therefore, it is useful to know different ways of storing it.

Pre-drying Treatment

Before drying your pumpkin in trays, indoors or out, you should give them the following pre-drying treatment to prevent spoilage, as pumpkins are a low-acid fruit. It is best to start with pumpkins brought directly from your garden rather than those that you have been storing. Select a mature deep orange pumpkin for drying.

To steam-blanch your pumpkin, put several inches of water in a good-sized kettle with a lid, which seals well. Suspend a wire basket or steamer in the pot above the water. Put in a layer of sliced pumpkins (slices should be approximately 1/8" - 1/4" thick.) You can leave the rind on the pumpkin if you like, or remove after you have sliced it as it will be easier than trying to remove it from the whole pumpkin first. Your slices should not be more than 2" deep for each blanching. Steam-blanch the slices for approximately six (6) minutes, or until slightly soft.

Remove the pumpkin, spreading it out on paper toweling or clean cloths to remove excess moisture. Cover it with extra toweling until you are ready to put it in the drying trays.[1]

Using a Dryer

Load your drying trays with shallow layers of the blanched pumpkin. Start the dryer at 140° F., increasing the temperature to 160° F. by the end of the first hour. Reduce the temperature to 130° F. when the pumpkin seems nearly dry. After it is dry, pasteurize the pumpkin. You do this by preheating your regular oven to 175° F. and loosely spreading the pumpkin not more than 1" deep on the trays. Do not try to do more than two trays at a time. Heat the pumpkin in the oven for 10 minutes. Remove from the oven and cool on clean cloth or paper toweling.[2]

Sun Drying

Prepare the pumpkin by the blanching method. Put on trays or screens and take outdoors. You may need to cover your screens with cheesecloth or more screening to protect them from insects. Test the slices for dryness daily, turning them at least once. Bring them inside when dry and pasteurize them.

To store your dried pumpkin, pack it into plastic bags or cartons. If you use bags, squeeze the air out before closing them. Tie them tightly around the top. Store the containers in a cool, dry place, preferably out of the sunlight. Six months is a good amount of time to store your dried pumpkin to get maximum nutritional benefit from it. When you are ready to use it for making flour, you will simply take it and grind it in a food processor.[3]

Using Dried Pumpkin

You can reconstitute the dried pumpkin by soaking it in hot water or cider. One half cup of hot liquid used with 1/2 cup of pumpkin will yield approximately 3/4 cup of soft pumpkin that you can then mash or use as is in your recipes.

Another use for your dried pumpkin is making pumpkin flour. Pioneers, often lacking wheat, would dry pumpkin and make flour out of it. You will handle it slightly differently. I used a small pumpkin (about 5 - 6 pounds). Wash the pumpkin and remove the top and stem. Slice the pumpkin in half and remove the seeds and strands. Slice the halves into lengthwise wedges, which you then slice into thin strips about 1/4" thick. Put the slices in a pan, cover them with water and boil them briefly until somewhat soft.

Remove from the water and lay on paper towels, patting dry with more towels on top. Place in a food dryer and follow the directions above under Using a Dryer. When the pumpkin is completely dry, crumble it and place it in a grain mill. Grind it, putting it through the mill twice to increase the fineness of the grind. Pumpkin flour can be used to replace some of the flour in any recipe that uses flour, and it will add good color and moisture to the food.

Freezing

Wash the pumpkin, remove the seeds, and cut the flesh into pieces without peeling it. Precook it until tender in sufficient boiling water to cover it. You can also steam it or bake it in the oven at 350°. If you are using cooking in a pan in water or steaming it, when it is tender, remove from the water and drain. If you are baking it, remove from the oven. Lay the pieces out and cool them on flat trays or paper towels. Scrape the pumpkin from the rind when cool, put the pumpkin into a deep bowl or blender and mash it. You can freeze your pumpkin in almost any type of container as long as it seals tightly enough to protect it against loss of moisture and excessive exposure to air. When packing your pumpkin, leave 1/2" of headroom (1-1/2" for glass). Seal and freeze. It is best to use your pumpkin within six (6) months for maximum nutritional benefits.[4]

When you are making pumpkin pies, you might end up making more pumpkin pie mixture than you can use at one time. Pack the excess mixture into containers with enough for one pie in each container. Label the sealed containers and freeze. Thaw until it reaches its desired consistency before using.

Canning

The starch in pumpkins gradually changes to sugar as they age; you can use pumpkin flour as a natural sweetener in your bread recipe. No matter now you store your pumpkin, its water content will increase slightly.

Use pressure canning with a hot pack only. You should not use the boiling water bath canner except to make canned pumpkin pickles (the recipe uses a good amount of vinegar) and jams (the sugar achieves the preserving).

Pumpkin with slightly dry flesh will can best. If your thumbnail won't cut the skin readily, it's just right.[5]

Hot Pack Method for Cubes

Wash the pumpkin and cut into easy-to-handle pieces. Pare and remove the seeds. Cover with water in a large saucepan or kettle and bring to a boil. Drain, reserving the liquid, and pack jars while the fruit is hot.

Leaving 1/2" of headroom in each jar, add 1/2-tbsp. salt for pint-size jars and 1 tsp. for each quart. Carefully pour the cooking water into each jar, keeping the 1/2" of headroom. Adjust the lids. Pressure process pint jars for 55 minutes or quarts for 90 minutes at 10 lbs. (240° F.). Remove jars and tighten seals if necessary.[6]

Hot Pack Method for Strained Pumpkin

Prepare the pumpkin as before, but leave in larger pieces. Steam or bake until tender. Put through a sieve or food mill. Over a low heat, simmer until it is thoroughly heated, stirring constantly to prevent scorching. Pack the pumpkin into the jars while it is still hot, adding no additional liquid or salt. Again, leave 1/2" of headroom, but pressure-process pint jars for 65 minutes at 10 lbs. (240° F.), or 80 minutes for quarts. Remove jars and tighten seals if necessary.[7]

Your canned goods will keep better if they are stored in a cool, dark, dry place. Be sure to label them with dates so that you can use them within a year.

RECIPES

Note to readers: I purposefully don't always tell you how many people a recipe will serve here because if the recipe calls for a cup of pumpkin seeds, only you know whether you can sit there and eat the whole cup of seeds by yourself or not. If you can, then there will be none left for anyone else so you will need to keep increasing the recipe to make enough for all your folks. I always feel like such a piggy when the recipe calls for a certain amount that is supposed to feed four people and I end up eating all of it and feeling as though I had just enough for one person. I don't want you to have to feel like that. And then too, if you cook the way I do, you might just want to make extra whenever possible so you can save some for another snack or seconds, or even another meal. You can freeze many of the dishes. Think of it this way: Does 1 cup of anything sound like it will be enough to feed four people?

Also, when I tell you to use 1/2 tsp. nutmeg or cloves or ginger, I am ALWAYS referring to the ground forms of the spices. If I want you to use whole spices, I will so note. And finally, when I tell you to use salt, often I do NOT give you a measure for it. I think the use of salt is a very personal thing. I have made the same recipes WITH and WITHOUT it, and never saw any difference at all other than taste, and quite frankly, a recipe that calls for 1/4 tsp. salt or even 1/2 tsp. salt with large amounts of the other ingredients will barely even be noticed taste-wise. Now the other thing is that if there is no salt mentioned in the recipe, that means there was none called for originally. I found some interesting historical facts about the use of salt and its value.

In ancient times, because there was no refrigeration, meat especially, and other foods would spoil readily, and salt was a way to try to prevent that, and to cover the taste of those things that perhaps began to smell bad.

Salt was not available in all areas of the world, and hence its value increased via trade routes or "salt roads." Wars were fought for it, and some places in the world gained much fame for their salt. Many articles have been written on the importance of salt, and you can find a number of books on its production too. But since we are covering pumpkins and not salt, it will suffice to say that salt has different meanings for different people. I did not find a single problem when I omitted it, so let's figure it is a very personal thing, and perhaps a symbolic one as well when cooking. Use your own judgment.

I have tried to write most of these recipes so that they are clear and concise for your benefit (and mine). I hope after reading the improved recipes, you'll chuckle the next time you read an instruction somewhere that reads, "Heat the butter in the pan until melted." Pray tell, how else would you heat the butter?

I have to tell you too that in general I am NOT a precise cook. I created precise measurements because you would go crazy if everything were not more or less measurable. But when I cook, I am pretty creative and seldom make the same recipe the same way twice. I will change the amounts and types of spices, or I will perhaps leave something out that doesn't feel right to me for that cooking session, or perhaps I will add something just because it seems like a good idea at the time. So don't hesitate to change things some if it feels right. Recipes seldom come out wrong as long as you cook them the right length of time and pretty much in the proportions given. I felt validated when a very good friend who was instrumental in my very earliest work on this book showed me some antique cookbooks from South Africa, and none of those had any precise measurements for anything.

Tummy Ticklers

Pumpkin Trail Mix

1 c. each pumpkin seeds, soy nuts, sunflower seeds and blanched almonds
2 tbsps. Tahini
1 tbsp. Honey
1 tsp. poppy seeds
1 tsp. vanilla
1/4 tsp. each powdered ginger and nutmeg
3/4 tsp. cinnamon
1-1/2 tsp. sesame salt (see below)

Preheat oven to 250°. Combine the first 4 ingredients. Mix remaining ingredients, then add to the nut mixture. Place in a shallow pan and bake until golden brown, shaking pan frequently. You can put some of the sesame salt (recipe below) on it for a really wonderful taste.

Sesame Salt

1 c. toasted sesame seeds
2 tsp. sea salt

Place ingredients in a grinder or blender and mix until the texture is fine. Store in a tightly closed container. This salt is also good on vegetables and salads.

Pumpkin Munchies

1 c. fresh pumpkin, thinly sliced
1 tbsp. Curry powder
1 tsp. garlic salt
1 tsp. parsley

Soak pumpkin slices in ice water for one hour. Drain and pat dry, then fry in hot oil (350°) until golden brown. Drain on paper. Combine curry, garlic salt and parsley, sprinkling over chips until thoroughly coated.

Peppery Curry Pumpkin Snacks

Pumpkin seeds are used in West Africa mainly for thickening soups or sauces, but on occasion, they are eaten as a snack food.

1 c. pumpkin seeds
1-1/2 c. water
Peanut or olive oil
1/4 tsp. chili pepper
1 tsp. curry powder
1/2 tsp. sea salt

Bring water to a boil and add seeds. After boiling for a few minutes, reduce heat and continue to simmer for 1/2 hour. Drain and dry seeds. Heat oil in a medium-size frying pan. Mix seeds, chili pepper, curry powder and salt. Heat them in the oil, shaking them frequently until they are thoroughly coated. Line shallow pans with paper such as that of paper bags and spread the seeds. Bake at 250° for 20 - 30 minutes or until golden brown, shaking the pan occasionally.

Curried Pumpkin Seeds

2 c. hulled pumpkin seeds
1/4 c. curry powder
1 c. warm water
Juice of one lime
1 clove of garlic, minced
1 tsp. sea salt
1 tbsp. butter or margarine.

Preheat oven to 225°. Mix curry powder, a little of the warm water, garlic, salt and lime juice until you have a smooth consistency. Add the remaining water and stir constantly over medium heat until the liquid begins to simmer. Add the pumpkin seeds and continue to simmer for five additional minutes. Drain and dry the seeds. Spread them on a baking sheet and dot with butter and salt. Roast until crisp, shaking the pan infrequently.

Toasted Pumpkin Seeds

2 c. pumpkin seeds
1 tbsp. melted butter, margarine or oil
salt

Preheat oven to 250°. Mix seeds, butter and salt in a small bowl. Spread seeds in a shallow baking pan and place in the center of the oven for 20 - 30 minutes, or until golden brown. Shake frequently during baking. Test the seeds frequently after 20 minutes to avoid overcooking. Serve warm or cool.

Pumpkin Milkshake

1 c. whole milk
1 whole egg
1/2 c. pumpkin
1/2 scoop vanilla ice cream
1/2 tsp. nutmeg or allspice
1 tbsp. honey

Mix ingredients in electric blender until smooth. You can sprinkle a little nutmeg or allspice on the top. If you are on a diet that won't allow you to have ice cream, you can still have a shake. Simply freeze the 1/2 c. of pumpkin, use low-fat milk, and . Put the frozen pumpkin in the blender with the milk, spice, egg, and honey and mix until smooth.

Pumpkin Seed Cooler

1 c. chilled, canned pineapple juice
1/4 c. hulled pumpkin seeds
1/4 c. sunflower seeds

Combine ingredients in blender and whip for 1 minute, or until smooth. You can vary this recipe by substituting apple or tomato juice, and adding a spring of parsley and 1/4 tsp. of basil.

Winter Health Tea

1/3 tbsp. pumpkin seeds, hulled
1/3 tbsp. fragrant valerian root
1/3 tbsp. bilberry leaves

Mix ingredients and steep in 1 cup of boiling water. Drink the tea unsweetened over the course of a day. This tea is thought to be helpful for those with diabetes or hypoglycemia.

Pumpkin Sandwich

2 slices wheat or wholegrain bread
1 small wedge of pumpkin, steamed and sliced thin
Lettuce leaves (enough for a sandwich)
1 tsp. chives or green onions, finely chopped
Mayonnaise

Spread bottom piece of bread with mayonnaise and pumpkin slices sprinkled with salt and chives or green onions. Add lettuce and second piece of bread.

Pumpkin Sandwich with Dates, Raisins and Cream Cheese

2 slices wheat or wholegrain bread
1 small wedge of pumpkin, steamed
6 sun-dried dates, finely chopped
1/4 tsp. each cinnamon, nutmeg (you can also use 1/4 tsp. allspice if you like)
1 tbsp. seedless raisins
Lettuce leaves
Adequate cream cheese to spread on bread

Spread cream cheese on bottom slice of bread. Mash pumpkin and mix with dates and raisins. Spread thickly over the cream cheese. Add lettuce. Sprinkle with seasonings and add second piece of bread.

Pumpkin Sandwich with Peanut Butter and Cranberry Sauce

2 slices wheat or wholegrain bread
1 small wedge of pumpkin, steamed and sliced thin
Peanut butter (I prefer crunchy)
Cranberry Sauce from can

Spread peanut butter, slices of pumpkin, and cover with cranberry sauce over bottom slice of bread according to the amount you like. Cover the bread and you are probably going to want another one.

Pumpkin Hummus

I discovered pumpkin hummus one Thanksgiving in a local natural food store. One container and I was hooked, but didn't want to wait for another Thanksgiving before I had more. This is a refreshing snack even during the heat of summer.

1 lg. can pumpkin
2-1/2 tsps. Tahini
2 tbsps. lemon juice
1-1/2 tsp olive oil
1 tsp ground cumin
1/2 tsp. ground red pepper, salt
1 tsp. chopped garlic
2 tbsps. fresh parsley, chopped finely
6 (6-inch) pitas, each cut into 8 wedges

Place ingredients in the blender and blend until smooth. Put into serving dish and add chopped parsley, stirring until fully blended. Put in refrigerator and cool.

Preheat oven to 425°. Place pita wedges on cookie pan and bake for approx. 5 minutes until light golden brown. Serve with hummus. You can also serve fresh cut vegetables with this. This is particularly good with chilled white wine such as Sauvignon Blanc.

Pumpkin Cheese Dip

1/2 c. canned pumpkin
8 oz. cream cheese
1 c. sour cream
1-1/2 c. cheddar cheese, shredded
1/3 c. chopped green onions
2 tsps. powdered chili
1 tsp. garlic salt

Combine canned pumpkin, cream cheese and sour cream in a large bowl, stirring until smooth. Add in remaining ingredients, stirring until well blended. This can be served with crackers or small rounds of crisp bread.

Fried Pumpkin Blossoms

3 dozen pumpkin blossoms
2 well-beaten eggs
1/2 c. flour
adequate oil to deep fry blossoms
1 tbsp. dried parsley, chopped
Salt and pepper

Gather blossoms before they are open. Remove stems, washing and draining blossoms on a paper towel. Make a batter out of eggs, flour, salt, pepper and chopped parsley.

Dip blossoms into the batter and immerse carefully in the hot oil (375°), frying until golden brown. Drain on absorbent paper. It goes well with ham or pork and applesauce. It also makes a delicious side dish for breakfast (omit parsley, salt and pepper and serve with butter and syrup, or powdered sugar and lemon juice). Sprinkle a little cinnamon on them if you like.

Soups & Salads

Chicken or Turkey Stock for Soups

Extra chicken pieces from 2 chickens (backs, necks, and wings) or 1 turkey leg, wings, and neck will do
2 stalks celery chopped and including chopped celery tops
2 sliced carrots
1 large sliced onion
Salt and pepper
1 tsp. Italian seasoning
6 c. cold water

Put all ingredients into large kettle or pot and bring to boil. Reduce heat and simmer for 1 hour. Remove chicken or turkey, strain stock and save vegetables and chicken or turkey for another use. If you are using the stock right away, skim off fat before using. If you are not using the stock right away, you can chill and lift off fat easily. Makes approx. 4 1/2 cups stock. Note: If a recipe calls for a ham stock, you would make it the same way using ham hocks or ham neck bones. And of course you can used packaged or canned Chicken or turkey stock instead of making it yourself.

Sunshine Soup

3 c. steamed and mashed pumpkin
5 c. chicken or turkey stock
Salt and pepper
1 c. unsweetened and whipped heavy cream
2 c. light cream

1 c. chopped onion
8 thin slices tomatoes
1/2 c. chives

In a large pot, combine pumpkin, chicken broth and onion. Bring to a boil, stirring frequently. Simmer for 10 minutes and then cool. Stir light cream into soup and add seasonings. Pour soup into chilled cups and float tomato slices. Spoon whipped cream onto each slice and sprinkle with chives. Serves 4 unless everyone is very hungry.

Curried Pumpkin Soup

3 c. mashed pumpkin
4 c. water
1/4 c. butter or margarine
1 sm. onion, sliced thinly
1 c. coconut milk
1/2 c. quick cooking rice
1 tbsp. curry powder
1/2 tsp. ea. coriander and cinnamon
Salt and pepper
Fresh mint, chopped fine

Sauté onion in butter until golden brown. Add pumpkin, rice (and) water, blending thoroughly. Bring to a boil, then simmer for approx. 5 minutes, or until rice is cooked thoroughly. Stir constantly while simmering. Add coconut milk and sprinkle mint over top just before serving. This is generally good for 2 people.

Vegetable Soup with Pumpkin

2 c. fresh pumpkin, cubed
2-1/2 quarts chicken or turkey stock
3 quarts water
4 carrots, sliced
2 potatoes, cubed
2 turnips, diced
2 stalks celery, diced
2 sm. onions, thinly sliced
1 c. ea. corn, lima beans
1/2 tsp. ginger
Salt and pepper

Put all ingredients into a large kettle and bring to a boil. Turn heat down and continue to simmer 1 hour, or until vegetables are soft enough to suit your taste. Serves 4 if you are not making this a main course. If you are, you might want to double your recipe and serve some good hot bread and a salad with the soup.

Country Pumpkin Soup

1 sm. (approx. 5 lbs.) pumpkin with solid stem
6 c. turkey or chicken stock
2 c. bread crumbs
1/2 c. ea. fresh coarsely grated Swiss and Parmesan cheese
1 c. heavy cream
6 tbsp. butter
1 tsp. ground nutmeg
Salt and pepper
1 c. finely chopped chives
Finely chopped fresh parsley

Preheat oven to 350°. Spread breadcrumbs in a shallow baking pan and dry in the oven for about 15 min., shaking pan once or twice. Remove pan and increase oven heat to 375°.

Cut off a good lid on the pumpkin, saving the top. This top should be wide enough to easily reach your hand comfortably into the pumpkin to scrape out the seeds and stringy material, but not too large. Save the lid too.

Heat butter in a skillet and add the chives, cooking them just slightly. Add the spices. Remove from the heat and stir in the cheeses, then spoon the mixture into the pumpkin. Add turkey stock, leaving 1" at top of pumpkin. Place bay leaf on top of filling and replace cover.

Place pumpkin in lightly oiled baking dish and cover sides of pumpkin with aluminum foil. Bake 1 hour, or until the pumpkin begins to soften and soup is bubbling. Reduce oven heat to 300° and bake 30 additional minutes, or until pumpkin is tender but still holds its shape well.

Before serving, remove pumpkin lid, remove bay leaf, and stir in cream and chopped parsley. Serve soup with a little of the pumpkin flesh scraped from inside for each serving. Serves 6, but if it is to be a main dish, you might want to serve a salad and a good hot bread with it.

Caldito Calabasas

3 c. mashed pumpkin
5 c. chicken or turkey stock

1 c. chopped fresh tomatoes
1 c. chopped onion
1/2 c. cilantro
4 tbsps. butter or margarine
2 c. light cream
1/2 tsp. ea. allspice, coriander, and mace
Salt and pepper

Sauté onion in butter. Add 1 cup of the chicken stock and seasonings and bring to a boil. Reduce heat and simmer, covered, for 5 minutes. Remove from heat and add cream, pumpkin and remaining chicken broth. Stir to blend. Heat gently until very hot, but do not boil. Garnish with chopped tomatoes and cilantro. Serves 4, but if you want it to be the main course, make more or serve a salad and some hot bread with it. You can also have some sour cream available at the table in case anyone wants to put a dollop in the soup.

Middle Eastern Pumpkin Soup

3 c. cubed and peeled pumpkin
1-1/2 c. dry garbanzo beans
2 white turnips, diced
2 carrots, thinly sliced
3 ears of corn, cut into 2" pieces
2 c. diced tomatoes
1 beef stock bone
1-1/2 lb. Cubed boneless beef
1 ham hock
4 qt. Water
1 tsp. oregano
4 garlic cloves, chopped

Salt and pepper
Cilantro sprigs

Combine beans and 3 c. water in a large kettle, soaking overnight. Add remaining water, meat and bones, seasonings and garlic and bring to a boil. Cover and simmer for 1 hour or until meat is tender. Add pumpkin and other vegetables (except corn) and simmer for 20 more minutes or until vegetables are tender. Add corn, cover and simmer for 10 more minutes. Remove beef and ham bones from soup. Garnish each serving with a sprig of cilantro. Might serve 6 if you are not making it a main course, or no one asks for seconds. Some pita bread would be a good accompaniment.

Burmese Soup

3 c. peeled and thinly sliced pumpkin
2 sm. onions, thinly sliced.
2 stalks celery, diced
2 jalapeno peppers, seeds removed and sliced (be very careful to wear gloves and make sure not to touch your eyes while preparing any hot peppers)
1-1/2 c. mushrooms
2 lemons, sliced thinly
1 c. chopped Thai basil (if you cannot get the Thai basil, you can use regular basil)
2. c. raw shrimp, shelled and deveined
5 c. chicken stock
1 tsp. ea. ground caraway and cinnamon
Salt and pepper

Cut shrimp into bite-sized pieces and place in medium pan.

Add stock, seasonings, celery, garlic, jalapeno peppers and onions. Bring to a boil, then add pumpkin and simmer 15 minutes more, or until pumpkin is tender. Serve with basil and lemons. Serves 4, but if you want it as a main dish, make more or serve with salad.

This recipe would be really delicious with Burmese bread, a little flat round bread made of dried ground chickpea flour. It looks like pita bread but has red onion, chili and cilantro in the dough. The bread is also served with various dipping sauces. If you cannot get the Burmese bread, you can substitute pita or other wholegrain flatbread and any good dipping sauce that appeals to you.

Japanese Pumpkin Soup

3 c. pumpkin, peeled and sliced thinly
1 medium potato, peeled and sliced thinly
1 c. ea. chopped sorrel and spinach
1 c. green peas
1 sm. leek, thinly sliced
1 c. chopped lettuce
1-1/2 c. cooked rice
4 c. water
4 c. heavy cream
4 tbsps. minced fresh parsley
1 tsp. sweet basil

Place pumpkins, potato slices and seasonings in a saucepan; add water and bring to a boil. Turn heat down and continue to simmer until tender. Put cooked vegetables, together with liquids, through blender until smooth. Stir cream into puree.

Sauté lettuce, spinach, sorrel and leek in butter until tender, but not browned. Add vegetables and rice to soup. Add vegetables and rice to soup. Simmer soup for 10 minutes, stirring occasionally. Garnish with parsley. Serves 4 if it isn't your dinner; otherwise make more. This is a somewhat delicate flavored soup so keep that in mind if you are selecting other dishes to go with it.

Golden Pumpkin Soup

1-1/2 lbs. Pumpkin, peeled and cut into small pieces
3 sm. sweet potatoes, peeled and cut into small pieces
1 lg. onion, chopped
4 celery stalks, sliced
2 sprigs ea. fresh thyme and basil, leaves only and cut fine
salt and pepper
1 tbsp. olive oil
1 tbsp. butter or margarine
1 c. white wine
7-8 c. chicken broth

In a kettle or large pot, melt the olive oil and the butter together. Add the onions and the celery, and cook over medium heat until they are soft but not colored. Add the white wine and simmer 3 – 4 minutes. Add the pumpkin, sweet potato, chicken stock and seasonings and simmer for 30 minutes, or until pumpkin and sweet potato are soft. Remove and drain 2 cups of the vegetables and set aside. Purée the rest of the soup using a blender or food processor. When the purée is completed, stir in the reserved vegetables. Serves 4 if not intended as a main dish. Certainly more white wine would be good, along with some good thick, hot French bread and perhaps a light salad.

Old English Soup

4 c. cooked and pureed pumpkin
7 c. ham broth
1 tbsp. Worcestershire sauce
3 lg. Cloves garlic, minced
Salt and Pepper
1 tsp. Bovril (beefy extract that also comes in a vegetarian formula). This extract is available in 4 oz. Jars for about $7.00. It is very salty, so use sparingly. If you have a salt restriction in your diet, this recipe might not be a wise choice.

Combine all ingredients in a large kettle and place over medium heat, stirring until blended and good for serving.

To make this soup into a cream soup, omit the Worcestershire sauce, the garlic and Bovril. For liquid, use only 4 c. ham broth and add 1 c. tapioca. Heat until the broth reaches a boil. Lower heat and add pumpkin garlic and pepper, stirring until blended thoroughly. Combine 1 c. heavy cream with 1 c. milk and 1 tbsp. brown sugar in a separate saucepan and bring to a boil with 1 tbsp. brown sugar. Lower heat, add pumpkin and ham broth mixture, and simmer for 10 minutes more, stirring frequently. Season with a sprinkling of nutmeg in each bowl. Serves 4 if not a main dish. A good multi-grain bread or roll would be good with this soup. It is a very good winter soup.

Jamaican Pumpkin Soup

4 c. peeled pumpkin
5 c. chicken broth
1 c. coconut milk
8 ounces cubed pork
1 lg. onion, chopped
2 cloves garlic, minced
2 tsps. minced fresh ginger
2 tbsps. powdered hot chile pepper
1 lg. bay leaf
1 sprig ea. thyme and basil, leaves only, chopped
1 tsp. ground allspice
salt and pepper.

Combine all ingredients in large kettle or saucepan. Bring to boil; reduce heat, cover and simmer for 30 minutes or until pumpkin is soft. Turn heat off and remove pork and bay leaf. Purée soup in blender or food processor until smooth. Return to pot, add pork and reheat. Serves 4 if not a main dish. Jamaicans sometimes serve fruited breads with meals; two you might consider for this dish would be banana bread or cherry bread.

Cold Pumpkin Soup With Almonds

4 c. cooked, mashed pumpkin
1/4 c. chopped almonds
1 sm. onion, finely diced
4 c. chicken or turkey broth
4 tbsp. butter or margarine
2 tbsps. sherry
1 tbsp. fresh chopped parsley
Salt and pepper

Sauté onion in butter in skillet until golden. Add pumpkin, almonds and broth in a kettle, bringing to a boil. Reduce heat; cover and simmer 30 minutes, stirring occasionally. Add salt, pepper and sherry turn off heat. Chill for 1 hour before serving. Sprinkle fresh chopped parsley over each bowl. Serves 4 if not a main dish. This is a wonderfully refreshing summer or spring dish.

Cold Pumpkin Soup, Version II

1 lg. can pumpkin
2 lg. tomatoes, diced
2 medium carrots, peeled and chopped
1/2 c. celery, chopped
2 c. chicken broth
1-1/2 c. heavy cream
1 tbsp. butter
2 tbsps. honey
1 tbsp. ea. fresh basil, thyme and rosemary
Salt and pepper

Combine the vegetables, herbs and chicken stock and cook slowly in a covered saucepan until the vegetables are tender. Cool and puree the vegetables with the liquid. Combine with cream, butter, and honey and simmer, stirring constantly until soup is starting to bubble. Remove from heat, cool and then chill. You can serve this with dollops of sour cream and good hot French or other favorite bread and a green salad for a nice summer meal.

Pumpkin Soup With Gruyere Cheese

One 4 - 5 lb. fresh pumpkin
1 c. croutons
1 tbsp. ginger
1/2 sweet yellow onion, sliced thin
5 c. chicken or turkey stock
1/4 c. Orange Juice
1/2 c. cream sherry
1 c. heavy cream
2 tbsps. butter or margarine
6 ounces grated Gruyere Cheese
Salt and pepper

Preheat oven to 350°. Spread bread crumbs in a shallow baking pan and dry in the oven for about 15 min., shaking pan once or twice. Remove pan and increase oven heat to 375°.

Cut off a good lid on the pumpkin, saving the top. This top should be wide enough to easily reach your hand comfortably into the pumpkin to scrape out the seeds and stringy material, but not too large. Save the lid too.

Heat butter in a skillet and add the onion, cooking until golden. Add the ginger. Remove from the heat and stir in remaining ingredients, sprinkling cheese on top. Leave 1" at top of pumpkin.

Place pumpkin in lightly oiled baking dish and cover sides of pumpkin with aluminum foil. Bake 1 hour, or until the pumpkin begins to soften and soup is bubbling. Reduce oven heat to 300° and bake 30 additional minutes, or until pumpkin is tender but still holds its shape well.

Before serving, remove pumpkin lid. Serve soup with a little of the pumpkin flesh scraped from inside and garnish each bowl with croutons. Serves 6, but if it is to be a main dish, you might want to serve a salad and a good hot bread with it.

Pumpkin-Apple Soup

4 c. pumpkin, cooked and mashed
2 c. apples, peeled and diced
1 sm. onion, diced
4 c. chicken or turkey broth
2 c. light cream
2 tbsp. butter or margarine
1 tsp. ea. cinnamon, nutmeg and allspice

Put butter and onion in skillet and cook until golden. Turn off heat and put onion and remainder of ingredients into large saucepan or kettle. Bring to a boil, then turn down and simmer until apples are tender, stirring frequently. Serves 4 if not used as a main dish. This dish would also be good as a summer dish if served chilled.

Yummy Pumpkin Soup

1 med. size pumpkin (5 - 6 lbs.) cut open, seeds and membranes removed, and peeled
1 c. vanilla soy milk for every cup of pumpkin puree (Instructions follow)
2 tsp. cinnamon and 1/4 tsp. nutmeg for each cup of soy milk used

Cut one medium size pumpkin into approximately 4" squares, and steam until soft (45 minutes approx.) Press the pumpkin through a wire mesh strainer or an apple sauce maker if you have one. You want only smooth pumpkin puree. (You can use canned if you must, but the soup won't taste nearly as good. Also, if you use canned pumpkin, you will have approx. two cups of pumpkin.) Measure the pureed pumpkin. For every cup of pumpkin puree, add one cup of vanilla soy milk and heat to nearly boiling. Remove from heat and combine pumpkin, hot soymilk, and 2 tsp. cinnamon and 1/4 tsp. of nutmeg for each cup of soymilk used. Whisk with a wire whisk until smooth and creamy. For a thicker soup, use less soymilk. This soup is low fat, healthy, and simple. It's good served cold as well. *Recipe courtesy of Shoshona Jemison Edwards.*

Cream of Pumpkin Soup

4 c. pumpkin, cooked and mashed
1 small onion, sliced thin
2 c. milk
1 c. heavy cream
2 c. chicken or turkey stock
1 egg yolk
2 tbsp. flour
2 tbsp. butter or margarine
1/2 tsp. ea. marjoram, sweet basil, and parsley
1 tsp. paprika
1/2 tsp. garlic salt
2 tbsp. sherry

Sauté onion in a skillet in butter until golden. Remove from heat and put in a kettle or large saucepan. Add flour, spices (except paprika) and butter and blend medium heat. Add chicken or turkey stock a little at a time and then add milk, but not cream. Cook until it bubbles around the edge and then add pumpkin and simmer about 15 min., stirring constantly. Just before serving, beat the egg yolk, heavy cream and sherry together in a small bowl. Stir tablespoonfuls of soup into the mixture until there are about four tablespoonfuls; then stir the mixture back into the soup. Cover and let cook until soup is the consistency of thick cream. Sprinkle paprika over each serving. Serves 4 if not used as a main dish.

Pumpkin Soup Virginian

4 c. diced, peeled pumpkin
3 carrots, diced
3 turnips, diced
3 stalks celery, chopped
1 sm. onion, finely chopped
5 c. chicken or turkey broth
1 c. heavy cream
1 c. milk
2 c. diced ham
1 tsp. ea. nutmeg, allspice and ground ginger
1 tbsp. brown sugar

Place pumpkin, carrots, turnips, celery, onion, bay leaf and broth in a large kettle or saucepan. Bring to a boil. Lower heat, cover and simmer for about 40 min., or until pumpkin and other vegetables are tender and remove from heat, remove bay leaf. Put mixture through food processor or in blender and blend until smooth. Stir in remaining ingredients except milk. Add milk last, stirring until consistently smooth. Serves 4 unless used as a main dish. This is one of those smooth soups that is very satisfying with almost any autumn meal.

Bean and Pumpkin Soup

2-1/2 lbs. Pumpkin, peeled and cubed (this is around half a small (4-5 lb. pumpkin)
1/2 lb. ea. dried lentils and navy beans
1 ham hock
2 qts. water
1 c. medium chopped onion
3 stalks celery, chopped
1/2 tsp. basil, marjoram, thyme
1 bay leaf
Salt and pepper

Combine beans and water in a large kettle, cover and soak in the 2 qts. water overnight before cooking. Add remainder of ingredients and bring to boil. Reduce heat; cover and simmer for one (1) hour, or until beans are tender, but not mushy. Remove from heat and remove bay leaf. Serves 4 unless it is to be a main dish. If it is a main dish, serve bread and salad with it.

Chilled Pumpkin Soup with Grand Marnier

4 c. pureed, cooked pumpkin.
2 ea. carrots, turnips, potatoes, celery, and leaks, cubed
3 c. corn kernels
4 - 5 c. beef or ham soup stock

2 c. lt. Cream
1 tsp. ea. allspice, thyme, ginger, cinnamon
Salt and pepper
Finely chopped candied ginger
1 c. Grand Marnier

Combine soup stock and vegetables (except corn and pumpkin) and all seasonings except candied ginger) in kettle or large saucepan and bring to boil. Reduce heat and simmer for 45 minutes, or until all vegetables are tender. Turn off heat and put vegetables and stock in a food processor or blender. Return to pan and add pumpkin and corn. Reheat about 15 minutes over moderate heat but do not allow to boil. Allow to cool, then chill thoroughly. When ready to serve, add light cream and Grand Marnier and serve the soup with candied ginger sprinkled on top of each serving.

Pumpkin and Oyster Soup

4 c. pureed pumpkin
3 stalks celery, diced
1 sm. onion, chopped finely
1 sprig parsley, chopped fine
4 c. chicken stock
1 c. heavy cream
1-1/2 c. fresh or canned oysters with juice
3/4 c. white wine
6 tbsps. flour
3 tbsps. butter
salt and pepper.

Melt 2 tbsps. butter, stirring in celery and onion; sauté until tender. Stir in remaining butter and flour, adding a little flour at a time and blending well with the vegetables. Add mashed pumpkin, seasonings, and white wine. Heat until soup begins to bubble around edges. Turn off heat and put soup through blender until smooth. Return to heat and add cream, blending in well. Add oysters and any accompanying liquid and cook for about 5 minutes, or until the oysters are thoroughly heated. Serves 2 - 4.

Pumpkin Soup Grenada

4 c. pureed pumpkin
2 ea. medium carrots, onions, and beets, cubed
1 ea. medium green pepper and onion, chopped
6 c. chicken or turkey stock
1 c. lt. cream
3 tbsps. bacon drippings
2 tbsps. minced chives
1/2 tsp. dill weed
1 tsp. ea. cinnamon, nutmeg, ginger
2 bay leaves
2 sprigs parsley, finely chopped
Salt and pepper
1/2 c. dark rum
4 tbsps. sour cream

Put bacon drippings in a large skillet and melt over medium heat. Add vegetables and sauté until tender. Turn off heat and put vegetables, chicken stock and seasonings (except parsley) in a large kettle and simmer for 30 minutes or until vegetables are tender. Turn off heat and put into blender or food processor; blend at medium speed until you have a smooth consistency. Return soup mix to heat and add pumpkin and cream, stirring until smooth and even in color.

Bring slowly to a boil, then turn heat off. Just before serving, add rum, sprinkle parsley and add 1 tbsp. sour cream to each serving. Serves 4 if not intended as a main dish. This is a very pretty soup.

Spencer's Health Soup

This soup is named for the friend who inspired me to write the original version of this cookbook. I never made it the same way twice.

4 c. pureed pumpkin
4 c. vegetable stock (make this the same way as chicken or turkey stock at front of soup recipes, using only the vegetables)
3 c. soy milk
1 tbsp. soy flour
1/2 c. powdered milk
2 tbsps. olive oil
3 tbsps. baker's yeast
1 sprig parsley, finely chopped
sea salt

Mix wet ingredients in kettle or large saucepan and heat thoroughly. Pour out 1/4 c. liquid into measuring cup and stir in flour and baker's yeast until thoroughly blended. Return to mix and heat a few minutes more.

Bread and Pumpkin Soup

4 c. fresh pumpkin, peeled and cubed
2 c. croutons or dry bread cut into cubes
4 c. water

1/4 c. olive oil
1 tsp. ea. basil, marjoram, and thyme
3 cloves garlic, peeled and diced
1 sprig fresh finely chopped parsley
2 tsps. paprika

Add pumpkin, garlic and seasonings (except chopped parsley and paprika) to water in a large kettle or saucepan and bring to a boil. Turn heat down and continue to simmer with lid on for 25-30 minutes, or until pumpkin is tender. Turn off heat and put in blender or food processor, blending until smooth. Put soup mixture back into pan, add bread and heat a few moments longer. Add olive oil just before serving and sprinkle chopped parsley and paprika on top of each serving. Serves 4 if not used as a main dish.

Pumpkin Chestnut Soup

4 c. fresh pumpkin, cubed
1 lb. shelled chestnuts, sliced thinly
1 medium onion, sliced thinly
3 carrots, sliced thinly
3 stalks celery with tops, chopped
4 c. turkey or chicken stock
1 c. light cream
1 tbsp. flour
1 bay leaf
1 sprig parsley, chopped
Salt and pepper

Put pumpkin, chestnuts, onion, celery stalks and tops, and carrots into kettle or saucepan with turkey or chicken stock and seasonings. Bring to boil, then lower heat. Cover and simmer until vegetables are tender. Turn off heat, empty pan into food processor or blender and blend until smooth. Put soup mixture back into pan, blend milk and flour and add to soup mixture. Heat for 10 minutes, or until mixture is consistently hot. Garnish with parsley. Serves 4 if not intended as main dish.

Mexican Blossom Soup

20 - 24 pumpkin blossoms
1 sm. onion, chopped
4 c. chicken broth
Sprigs of cilantro, chopped
Salt and pepper

Pick blossoms in the morning, or use them fresh after buying them. Wash carefully and remove stems. Place them in ice water in the refrigerator until ready to use. Sauté onion in butter in skillet until tender. Turn heat off and put onion in kettle or saucepan with drained pumpkin blossoms, chicken broth and seasonings except cilantro. Simmer for 5 minutes and turn heat off. Sprinkle cilantro on top of each serving. Serves 4 if not intended as main dish.

Pumpkin Soup with Black Beans

1 lg. can pumpkin
1 sm. can black beans
1 c. light cream
2 c. chicken broth
1 medium onion, peeled and diced small
1/2 c. celery, diced

1/2 c. carrots, sliced about 1/2"
1 tbsp. melted butter
Salt and pepper

Drain and puree the beans and set aside. Combine chicken broth, onion, carrots and celery over low heat until vegetables are tender. Cool briefly. Puree the vegetables, saving the liquid. Add remaining ingredients and heat over med. heat, stirring frequently until soup just begins to bubble. This is very good with some good hot French bread and some red wine.

Pumpkin Peanut Butter Soup

4 c. canned pumpkin
2 c. sweet potatoes, pureed
1 c. peanut butter
1/4 lb.. butter
 4-1/2 c. chicken broth (canned)
salt and pepper
chives, chopped finely
Sour cream

Melt butter in a soup pot over medium heat. Stir in pumpkin, sweet potatoes and peanut butter. Add broth, pepper and salt and continue to stir until smooth. Reduce heat and simmer for 15 - 20 minutes. To serve, garnish with chives and sour cream.

Salad n' Seeds

1 c. ea. raw zucchini, raw cauliflower, chopped finely
1 raw beet, peeled and grated

2 lg. Tomatoes, diced small
1/2 c. raw mushrooms, sliced
8 lettuce leaves, shredded
3/4 c. raw pumpkin seed kernels, chopped

Add vegetables together in salad bowl and toss together. Sprinkle raw pumpkin seed kernels over each serving and serve with your favorite choice of dressings. Something with ginger would be very tasty. Serves 4 if not a main dish.

Autumn's Delights Salad

4 c. chopped lettuce
1/2 c. each shredded carrot and turnip
2 sticks celery, diced
1 avocado, thinly sliced
2 medium tomatoes, thinly sliced
1/2 c. alfalfa sprouts
2 hard-boiled eggs, thinly sliced
1/2 c. Monterey cheese, cubed
1/2 c. raw pumpkinseed kernels
1 tbsp. fresh chopped parsley
1 tsp. ea. basil and thyme
green pepper, sliced thinly
1/2 c. yogurt
4 tbsps. butter
1/2 tsp. ea. dry mustard, ground cumin, ginger, coriander and sea salt
Few sprigs of fresh mint

Put pumpkin, pepper and seasonings in a skillet and sauté until tender. Let cool and stir in yogurt. Garnish with mint and serve with cooked rice. Serves 2 – 4, depending on if you intend to use it as a meal.

Jellied Pumpkin Ring

2 c. mashed, cooked pumpkin (you can use canned pumpkin, not the pie filling)
1 pkg. Orange-flavored gelatin
1-1/2 c. water, boiled
2 tbsp. brown sugar
1 tsp. grated orange rind
1 teaspoon pumpkin pie spice
1 small tub Cool Whip
1/2 cup chopped pecans

Dissolve Jell-O in boiling water; add sugar and spice. Add pumpkin, mixing well. Chill until slightly thickened, then add Cool Whip and chopped pecans. Pour into mold and refrigerate. Serves 4 if not a main dish.

Apple-Pumpkin Salad

1 c. grated raw pumpkin, steamed until tender
1 c. diced apples
1/2 c. seedless raisins
1 raw green pepper, sliced thinly
Lettuce leaves (use any type you favor)
1 c. chopped salad
1 c. diced pecans
Mayonnaise or similar textured dressing
1 tsp. ea. ginger, nutmeg and cinnamon
1 tsp. paprika

Put vegetables and fruits (except lettuce) in salad bowl, stirring in several spoonful of mayonnaise. Add spices (except paprika) and serve on lettuce leaves. Sprinkle each serving with paprika. Serves 4 if not a main dish.

Roast Pumpkin Salad

1 small pumpkin, seeds removed, sliced and peeled
Spinach leaves, washed
1 c. fresh green beans, blanched in hot water (bring to a boil and immediately turn off heat and drain)
1 c. fresh asparagus, blanched
1 c. sundried tomatoes
Olive oil

Heat oven to 350°. Arrange pumpkin slices in a single layer in a large flat pan oiled with small amount of olive oil and bake until golden and tender. Set aside to cool. When cool, mix in green beans, asparagus, and sundried tomatoes. Serve on spinach leaves with a good oil and balsamic prepared dressing or your own special version. Serves 4 if not a main course.

Thai Pumpkin and Chicken Salad

2 c. raw, grated pumpkin
2 c. chopped coleslaw (I use the bagged mix with purple and green cabbage and carrots)
1/2 c. craisins (dried cranberries and raisins that you can purchase in the dry fruits section of your store)
1/4 c. green onion, chopped finely
2 chicken breasts
1 package oriental noodles
1/2 c. peanuts

Place noodles in saucepan and cover with water. Bring to boil and then lower heat and simmer for a few minutes. These noodles don't take but a few minutes, so keep testing to see if they are the right texture for you. When they are, turn off heat and drain. Put into deep salad bowl and set aside.

Cook chicken breasts in oven (350°) until done (about 30 min.) or I cook mine in the microwave, 3 minutes on each side for a single chicken breast. Just make sure they are thoroughly cooked. Cut up chicken.

Mix remaining ingredients in separate bowl and stir in chicken. Place over the noodles. Serve with a prepared sesame ginger or other oriental dressing. Serves 2 as a main dish.

Pumpkin Coleslaw

1/2 c. peeled and grated raw pumpkin
3/4 cup Granny Smith apple, grated or finely chopped
1/2 pkg. packaged coleslaw mix
1/3 cup mayonnaise
4 tbsps. apple cider vinegar
1 tbsp. brown sugar
salt

Combine pumpkin, apple and packaged coleslaw mix. In separate bowl, combine mayonnaise with vinegar and brown sugar, stirring well until thoroughly blended. Mix dressing into coleslaw.

Pumpkin Dressing

2 c. pumpkin
1 c. finely chopped green onion
1 c. sour cream
1 c. mayonnaise
1/4 c. honey
1/2 c. Dijon mustard
1/2 c. red wine vinegar
2 tbsps. garlic powder
Salt and pepper

Put all ingredients in blender and blend until smooth and creamy. Refrigerate until ready to serve on any salad of greens or greens with fresh vegetables.

Breads, Batters & Biscuits

Pumpkin Doughnuts

2 c. mashed pumpkin
3-1/2 c. flour
1 c. milk
1 egg
1 cake compressed yeast, crumbled (or 1 pkg. Dry yeast)
1/2 c. brown sugar, packed
1 tsp. ea. cinnamon, nutmeg, allspice and ginger
1 tsp. vanilla
Oil for frying
3 tbsps. butter or margarine
Powdered sugar (optional)

Dissolve yeast in 1/4 c. warm water. Heat milk until bubbles form around edge, and then remove from heat and add butter, salt and sugar. Cool until lukewarm, then add yeast mixture. Stir in pumpkin, egg, vanilla and spice. Add the flour, a cupful at a time, until you have a soft dough that is not sticky.

Roll out dough to 1/4" thick. Cut out 3" round doughnuts and place on floured baking sheet. Centers be cooked the same as the doughnuts themselves. Cover and let rise in a warm place (85 - 90° F.) until double in bulk. Fry in hot oil (3-4") until golden brown (1 - 2 minutes per side. Keep checking.) Drain on absorbent paper. You can also sift powdered sugar on them too if you like. Should make 10 - 12 doughnuts.

Pumpkin Beignets

After a visit to a Louisiana style restaurant where we had Beignets (a square shaped donut with no holes that is covered with powdered sugar) for breakfast, I decided to find a basic recipe and use pumpkin to create some for myself. This is a bad, bad recipe (NOT!). Plan on people eating about 3 - 4 each. It is very hard to stop once you get started.

1 c. canned pumpkin
7 cups all-purpose flour
2 eggs, beaten
1 cup light cream
1/4 cup butter, softened
1 package active dry yeast
1 1/2 cups warm water
1/2 cup granulated sugar
1 teaspoon salt (for this recipe, you might want the amount of salt specified)
oil for deep frying
powdered sugar

In large bowl, sprinkle yeast over the warm water; stir to dissolve and let stand for 5 minutes. Add sugar, salt, beaten eggs, and evaporated milk. Whisk or use electric mixer to blend thoroughly. Add 4 cups of the flour; beat until smooth. Add pumpkin and butter; gradually blend in remaining flour. Cover with plastic wrap and chill at least 4 hours or overnight. Roll out on floured board to 1/8-inch thickness. Cut into 2 1/2 to 3-inch squares. Deep fry at 360° for 2 to 3 minutes until lightly browned on both sides. Drain on paper towels and sprinkle generously with powdered sugar or roll in the powdered sugar (even better). If you are going to eat something like this, you might as well do it right.

You can cut and freeze your dough if you like, separating it with waxed paper between the layers in the container.

Molettes de Calabasas (Pumpkin Muffins)

2 c. mashed pumpkin
1/2 c. raisins
1/2 c. pecans or walnuts, chopped finely
3/4 c. warm milk
1 egg
2-1/2 c. flour
1/2 c. brown sugar, packed salt
1 tsp. baking powder
1 tsp. ea. cinnamon, nutmeg, allspice and ginger

Preheat oven to 425°. Mix pumpkin, milk and egg. When mixture is smooth, add dry ingredients, including spices. Stir in raisins and nuts. Pour into oiled muffin pans, filling halfway. Bake 25-30 minutes, or until golden brown. For another different treat, you could substitute ¾ c. drained blueberries for the raisins and omit the nuts. This recipe will yield about 6 normal size muffins.

Pumpkin Pancakes

2 c. cooked and mashed pumpkin
2 eggs, well beaten
2 c. milk
2 c. unbleached flour
1 tbsp. wheat germ

1/4 c. honey
3 tbsps. sunflower seeds
1 tsp. ea. cinnamon, nutmeg, allspice, ginger
sea salt

Combine dry ingredients in large mixing bowl. Add milk, eggs, oil, honey, pumpkin, spices and salt and stir until smooth. Cooked on a hot, oiled griddle or large frying pan, spooning out adequate batter to make the size pancakes you want. This recipe will yield about 2 servings of 2 - 3 medium-size pancakes each.

Pumpkin Nut Waffles

2 c. mashed pumpkin
2 eggs, separated
2 c. milk
1/2 c. melted margarine
1/2 c. chopped pecans or other favorite nuts
2-1/2 c. enriched flour
1/2 c. brown sugar, packed
1 tsp. ea. cinnamon, nutmeg, allspice, ginger
2 tbsp. baking powder
Salt

Mix dry ingredients well. Combine well beaten egg yolks, milk and margarine; pumpkin, nuts and spices and add to the dry ingredients, blending well. Beat 2 egg whites until stiff; fold gently into batter. Bake in preheated waffle iron until steaming ceases and waffle is a golden brown. Makes 4 - 6 medium size waffles.

Pumpkin Sunrise Pancakes with Maple Cider Syrup

1/2 can pumpkin
2 c. sifted flour
4 eggs, separated
1-1/2 c. light cream
1/4 c. butter melted.
2 tbsps. brown sugar
1-1/2 tsp. baking powder
1 tsp. cinnamon
1/2 tsp. ea. nutmeg, ginger, cloves
salt

Combine dry ingredients. Add milk, pumpkin, egg yolks and melted butter to dry ingredients, stirring until blended. Beat egg whites until stiff and fold into batter. Drop approx. 1/4. cupfuls onto hot griddle, spreading batter slightly. Turn pancakes when they are bubbly on the top and brown on the bottom. Serve with Maple Cider syrup, recipe below.

Maple Cider Syrup

Mix apple cider and syrup to your taste and simmer uncovered 15 min. until it is slightly thickened. Serve warm over the pancakes.

Pumpkin Blossom Fritters

20 - 24 pumpkin blossoms
2 eggs
1-1/4 c. milk
2 tbsps. melted butter

Cooking oil
1/2 tsp. salt
2 lemons, halved and cut into wedges (for squeezing)
Powdered sugar

Gather pumpkin blossoms early in the morning and keep them in ice water until ready to use. Wash, drain and pat dry. Combine dry ingredients. . Beat eggs well and add milk and melted butter. Stir flour in gradually to prevent lumps. Dip the blossoms in the batter, coating them thoroughly. Heat 3 - 4" cooking oil to 370° or until it is just bubbling, but not smoking. Dip blossoms in the oil carefully, frying them until they just turn golden brown. Drain on absorbent paper. Serve with lemon and a bowl of powdered sugar. If you prefer, you can just serve with maple syrup. This will serve 4 if you are not considering it the main dish.

Pumpkin Fritters

2 c. cooked, mashed pumpkin
3 beaten eggs
1 c. flour
Cooking oil
Salt

Combine dry ingredients. . Beat eggs well and stir flour in gradually to prevent lumps. Dip the blossoms in the batter, coating them thoroughly. Heat 3 - 4" cooking oil to 370° or until it is just bubbling, but not smoking. Put large tablespoonfuls of the pumpkin mix into the oil and fry them until golden brown. Drain on absorbent paper. Serve with maple syrup or lemons and powdered sugar as in above recipe.

Pumpkin Corn Fritters

1 c. canned pumpkin
1 c. cream style corn
1-1/2 c. flour
1/4 c. milk
1 egg
2 tbsp. butter, melted
1 tsp. baking powder
1 tsp. pumpkin pie spice
Salt

Combine corn, egg, flour, baking powder and salt. Add milk and butter, then mix spices with pumpkin and mix into corn batter. Drop into deep fat, watching until it turns brown on both sides. You have to turn it once one side is done. Drain on paper.

Pumpkin Apple Fritters

1 lb. can pumpkin
1-1/2 c. applesauce
1-1/2 c. Bisquick
4 eggs, beaten
1.2 c. brown sugar
1/2 c. butter
1 tsp. cinnamon
1/2 tsp. ea. nutmeg and ginger

Mix eggs, pumpkin, applesauce, sugar and spices. Stir in biscuit mix. Heat butter in skillet and pour into frying pan about 1/4 c. for each fritter. Fry until golden brown, turning once to brown the other side.

Raised Pumpkin Biscuits

2 c. cooked, mashed pumpkin
1 c. scalded milk (bring to a boil and cool to lukewarm)
2 eggs
1/3 c. melted butter
1/2 c. lukewarm water
2-1/2 c. sifted all-purpose flour
1 envelope dry yeast (or one cake compressed)
1/4 c. sugar
1/2 tsp. salt

Dissolve the yeast in the 1/2 c. lukewarm water, along with 1/4 c. flour and 1 tbsp. of the sugar. Set in a warm, dry place for 3/4 hour. Add 1 more cup of flour, all the remaining sugar, salt, melted butter, eggs and pumpkin. Then add the remaining flour alternating with the scalded milk, beginning and ending with the flour. Use only enough flour to make a soft but kneadable dough. Place dough in oiled bowl and cover. Set in a warm, dry spot, allowing to rise until double in bulk, about 1-1/2 hours. Stir dough down, turn onto a well-floured board on pastry cloth and sprinkle top of dough with flour. Shape into a ball and knead lightly 3 - 5 minutes. Divide dough in half and roll out, half at a time, to a thickness of 1/2". Cut dough into 2-1/2" rounds. Reroll leftover dough and cut. Place biscuits 1/2" apart on ungreased baking sheet. Cover with cloth, and set in a warm, dry place to rise for 1/2 hour. Heat oven to 425° and bake biscuits for 14 minutes, or until lightly browned on top. Makes 12 biscuits.

Golden Harvest Biscuits

1 c. cooked, mashed pumpkin
3/4 c. milk
1/3 c. butter
1-1/2 c. flour
3 tsps. baking powder
1/4 c. sugar
1 tsp. ea. cinnamon, nutmeg, allspice, and ginger
salt
1/2 c. pecans
1/2 c. raisins

Preheat oven to 450° F. Sift flour into mixing bowl. Stir in remaining dry ingredients. Cut in butter with a pastry blender until mixture is crumbly. Stir in pumpkin and milk to form a soft dough. Add pecans and raisins to dough and roll out on floured surface to 1/2-inch thickness. Cut out biscuits with biscuit cutter. Place on oiled baking sheet. Bake for 15 to 20 minutes. Makes 24 biscuits.

Pumpkin Scones

1/2 cup canned pumpkin
2 cups flour
1/3 cup buttermilk
1/2 cup cold butter
1/2 cup brown sugar
1 tsp vanilla extract
1/2 tsp ground cinnamon
1/2 tsp ea. nutmeg, cloves, ginger
1 tsp baking powder
1/4 tsp baking soda
salt
1/2 c. chopped walnuts or pecans

Mix all dry ingredients, then chop the butter into small pieces and mix in with the dry ingredients until they are crumb-like. Then add the buttermilk, vanilla, and nuts mixing until you have a good dough that holds together. Turn dough out onto a floured board and knead 4 - 5 times. Shape into a circle that is about 1/2" thick. Cut into six pie-shaped pieces and brush with egg glaze below, then sprinkle with powdered sugar.

Egg glaze

1 egg
2 tbsps. Milk

Put scones on oiled cookie sheet and bake in preheated oven at 375° for 15 - 20 minutes, or until toothpick inserted in center comes out clean. For some good variations, you could add 1/2 c. chocolate or butterscotch drops, raisins or currants, or cranberries.

Pumpkin Dumplings with Hot Blueberry Compote

2 c. cooked, mashed pumpkin
2 eggs, separated
1/2 c. scalded milk (bring just until bubbling on edge and turn off heat)
3 tbsps. butter
1/2 c. sugar
1-1/2 c. flour

Mix the pumpkin, boiled milk, flour, butter and sugar. Allow to cool. Beat the egg yolks into the mixture. Beat the egg whites until stiff and fold gently into the mixture. Drop by tablespoonfuls into your favorite soup or stew and allow them to steam over a simmering heat for 8-10 minutes. You should get 10 - 12 dumplings.

You can also add the dumplings to hot blueberry compote (recipe below) for a delicious dessert, recipe below. When you are going to make the compote, you should boil several cups of water in a saucepan and then cook the dumplings in the water, turning the water to simmer with the lid on. When they are done, you will add them into the hot blueberry compote.

Hot Blueberry Compote

2 cups (1 pound) fresh blueberries
1/3 c. sugar
1/2 c. water

Combine 1 c. blueberries, sugar and water in small, heavy saucepan. Simmer over medium heat until berries burst, stirring often, about 10 minutes. Add remaining 1 cup berries. Cook until compote coats spoon, stirring often, about 8 minutes. (Can be made up to 3 days ahead.) Cover and chill. When you are ready to serve, add the pumpkin dumplings and heat until both dumplings and compote are warm. You can serve it with whipped cream and it will serve 4 if no one asks for seconds. My mother used to make Blueberry Compote and it was always one of my favorite deserts.

Pumpkin Hush Puppies

1 c. mashed pumpkin
1 c. buttermilk
2 eggs
2 c. corn meal
2 c. flour
3 tbsps. brown sugar
salt
1 teaspoon baking powder
2/3 teaspoon baking soda

Preheat oven to 350°. Mix all ingredients and form into long, small cakes. Place on a flat baking sheet and bake 20 - 25 minutes or until golden brown. You could also fry your hush puppies if you prefer, dropping tablespoonfuls of the mixture into a deep fryer filled with hot oil of your choice (some people might like to use vegetable oil for example). You will still cook these like donuts until they turn golden brown.

You should be able to get a couple dozen good hush puppies out of this recipe. Hush puppies are traditionally served with catfish, but you could serve them with anything.

Johnny Cakes

3 c. mashed pumpkin
1-1/2 c. milk, scalded
1 egg, beaten
1 c. boiling water
1 c. yellow cornmeal
2 c. flour

2 tbsp. baking powder
1/2 c. brown sugar
Salt

Let the cornmeal stand in boiling water until it swells, about 2 minutes. Add the milk, stirring until smooth. Then add the pumpkin and the dry ingredients. Drop tablespoonfuls of batter on a well-oiled griddle or skillet, flattening with the spoon. Bake until bubbles begin to form all over, turn and bake on the other side until done. Serve with maple syrup.

Apple-Pumpkin Whole Wheat Muffins

1/2 c. cooked, mashed pumpkin (canned is fine)
1/2 c. shredded apple with skin
1/2 c. canned unsweetened pineapple juice
1 tsp. grated lemon plus 1 tbsp. lemon juice
2 eggs
1 c. whole wheat flour
1 c. unbleached flour
1/2 c. brown sugar
2 tbsps. baking powder
1/2 c. pumpkin seeds
1/2 tsp. baking soda
salt

Preheat oven to 375°. Mix dry ingredients together thoroughly. Blend remaining ingredients, adding all at once to the dry ingre-dients. Stir until thoroughly moistened. Divide among 12 lightly oiled muffin cups, baking 15 - 20 minutes, or until golden brown.

Pumpkin Raisin Nut Muffins

2 c. pumpkin
1/2 c. milk
1 egg, beaten
1/4 c. butter, melted
1-1/2 c. flour
1/2 c. flaxseed flour (if you do not have this you can just add 1/2 c. more of regular flour)
1/4 c. brown sugar
1/2 c. raisins
1/2 c. chopped walnuts or pecans
1 tsp. pumpkin pie spice
2 tsps. baking powder
1/2 tsp. baking soda
salt

Preheat oven to 400°. Mix the dry ingredients together thoroughly. Blend the remaining ingredients, adding all at once to the dry ingredients. Stir just until thoroughly moistened. Divide among 12 lightly oiled muffin cups, baking for 15 - 20 minutes, or until toothpick inserted in center comes out clean.

Pumpkin Pineapple-Orange Nut Muffins

1/2 c. canned pumpkin
1/2 c. crushed pineapple, well-drained
2 c. flour
1 egg, beaten
1/2 c. brown sugar
1/2 c. orange juice
1/4 c. milk
1/4 c. melted butter

2 tsps. baking powder
1/2 tsp. baking soda
salt
1 tsp. cinnamon
1/2 tsp. ea. nutmeg, ginger, cloves
2 tsp. grated orange rind

Mix all dry ingredients and stir in egg, milk, orange juice and pumpkin. Fill oiled muffin tins 3/4 full and bake in a preheated oven at 400° for 15 - 20 minutes, or until toothpick inserted in center of muffins comes out clean.

Pumpkin Cornmeal Muffins

1/2 c. canned pumpkin
2 eggs, beaten
1/2 c. milk
1/4 c. butter, melted
1 c. flour
3/4 c. cornmeal
34 c. brown sugar
2 tsps. baking powder
1/2 tsp. baking soda
salt
1 tsp. pumpkin pie spice

Mix dry ingredients and then add butter, milk, eggs, and pumpkin. Pour into oiled muffin pans and bake in preheated 425° for 20 - 25 minutes. I love anything cornmeal, and this is just delicious served with butter and you can put some honey or syrup on top when you serve it.

Pumpkinseed Fruit Bars

1/2 c. mashed pumpkin
2 eggs
1/2 c. yogurt
1 tsp. vanilla
1/4 c. wheat germ
1/2 c. rolled oats
1 c. whole wheat flour
1 c. unbleached flour
1/2 c. brown sugar
salt
1 tsp. each cinnamon, nutmeg, allspice
1/2 c. raisins
1/2 c. pitted dates, diced
1/2 c. pumpkin seeds, hulled

Preheat oven to 350°. Combine wheat germ, oats and flour. Add remaining ingredients until well blended. Pour into an oiled 9" square baking pan and sprinkle with additional pumpkinseeds. Bake 45 minutes, or until toothpick inserted in center comes out clean. Cool in pan; cut into 9 squares.

Pumpkinseed Crackers

1/4 c. pumpkin seeds, ground large bits
1/4 c. sesame seeds
1/2 c. whole wheat flour
1/2 c. unbleached flour
salt
1/4 c. water
1/4 c. oil

Combine all ingredients and knead until smooth, adding more flour if necessary. Roll out dough 1/4" thick on floured surface and cut into desired shapes. Put on flat baking sheet and bake at 350° 10 - 15 minutes or until crisp.

Rising Pumpkin Bread

1 c. cooked, mashed pumpkin
1/2 c. warm water
6 tbsps. margarine
4 c. flour
1 cake compressed yeast or 1 pkg. dry yeast
1/2 c. brown sugar, packed

Dissolve yeast in warm water. Add salt, sugar and half of the flour. Set aside for 1/2 hour. Add the mixture to the pumpkin. Stir in butter and remaining flour. Turn out onto floured board and knead about 5 - 7 minutes. Shape into a ball and put into an oiled round 8" layer cake pan. Let rise until doubled in bulk, then bake in 375° oven about 30 - 40 minutes, or until golden brown. Bread is done when you thump it and it has a hard sound. Remove bread from the pan and cool on a rack.

Land-of-Honey Pumpkin Bread

1 c. mashed pumpkin
1 c. milk
1/4 c. honey
2 egg yolks
1/4 c. margarine
1/4 c. each chopped walnuts and dates

1/2 c. dried apricots
3 c. flour
salt
1 tsp. cinnamon
1 tsp. ea. ground cloves, nutmeg, ginger, and cinnamon

Preheat oven to 350°. Soak dried apricots in hot water for 5 minutes, then drain and cool. Stir the honey and milk over medium heat until milk is scalded. Cool for 5 minutes, then add the butter. Cool another 10 minutes and beat in pumpkin and egg yolks. Add dry ingredients, stirring thoroughly. Fold in fruit and nuts. Turn batter into a buttered, floured bread pan and bake for one hour, or until toothpick inserted in the center comes out clean. Cool the bread in the pan for 15 minutes and turn out on a rack to cool. This bread is very good served with cream cheese.

Holiday Pumpkin Bread

2 c. mashed pumpkin
4 eggs
1 c. oil
1 c. dates, chopped
3-1/2 c. flour
1/2 c. sugar
1./3 c. water
1 tsp. each cinnamon, nutmeg, and allspice
2 tsp. baking soda
Salt

Combine pumpkin, eggs, oil, water and dates, mixing well. Add dry ingredients to pumpkin mixture and blend. Pour into 2 greased and floured 9" x 5" loaf pan. Bake at 350°

25 - 30 min. or until done when pricked with a toothpick. Cool thoroughly before slicing.

Jamaican Pumpkin Bread

1 c. mashed pumpkin
1 c. ripe crushed bananas
2 eggs
1/3 c. Jamaican rum
1/2 c. margarine
1/2 c. each candied cherries, coconut, chopped nuts
2 c. biscuit mix
salt
1/4 c. brown sugar, packed
1 tsp. each cinnamon, nutmeg, and allspice

Oil and flour 9" x 5" loaf pan. Combine margarine, eggs, rum, pumpkin and bananas. Add biscuit mix, sugar and spice, beating until smooth. Fold in cherries, coconut and nuts. Pour into pan and bake at 350° for 45 min. or until toothpick inserted in center comes out clean. Allow to cool thoroughly before slicing.

Pumpkin Peanut Bread

1 c. mashed pumpkin
1/3 c. chopped peanuts (raw and unsalted)
1-1/2 c. boiling water
1-1/2 c. cold water
1/4 c. warm water.
1/4 c. peanut butter
1 tbsp. honey
3 c. unbleached flour

1 c. millet meal
1/4 c. cornmeal
2 tbsps. dry yeast

Mix cornmeal and cold water in saucepan. Add boiling water. Stir over heat until thickened, then let stand until cool. Mix yeast with the 1/4 c. warm water and let stand until yeast begins to bubble. Add pumpkin and yeast to peanut butter, mixing thoroughly. Blend in cornmeal mixture. Add flour, millet meal and chopped peanuts, mixing well. Knead for 5 minutes and placed in 2 oiled and floured 9" x 5" loaf pans. Lightly coat surface of dough with oil and let rise for about 45 minutes. Place in 400° oven for 10 minutes, then reduce heat to 350°. Bake 1 additional hour, or until toothpick inserted in center comes out clean. Allow to cool thoroughly before slicing.

Cactus Pear Pumpkin Bread

1 c. sugar
1 c. cooked, mashed pumpkin
1/4 c. corn oil
2 eggs
3 c. flour, all purpose
1/2 tsp. baking powder
1 tsp. baking soda
Salt
1 tsp. cinnamon
1/2 tsp. nutmeg
1 c. cactus pears, cut in half and insides scooped out
1 c. chopped almonds
1/2 tsp. vanilla
1/2 tsp. almond flavoring

Cream sugar, oil; beat in eggs and pumpkin. Sift flour, baking powder, soda, salt and spices. Stir in cactus pears. Add flavorings and almonds and stir until well blended. Bake in 2 oiled, floured 9" x 5" loaf pans at 325° for 1 hour or until toothpick inserted in center comes out clean. Take out of oven and allow to cool thoroughly before slicing.

Pumpkin Piñon Bread

1-1/4 c. mashed pumpkin
3 eggs, lightly beaten
1/2 c. margarine, melted
1 c. roasted, shelled Piñon nuts (pine nuts)
3 c. flour
2 tbsp. baking powder
1 c. brown sugar, packed
salt
1 tsp. each cinnamon and nutmeg

Combine flour, baking powder and spices; stir in nuts. Mix together other ingredients and add flour mixture, blending thoroughly. Pour batter in 2 oiled, floured 9" x 5" loaf pans and bake at 325° for 1 hour or until toothpick inserted in center comes out clean. Take out oven and allow to cool thoroughly before

Pumpkin Chocolate Chip Bread

1 lg. can pumpkin
1/2 cup butter, softened
3/4 cup brown sugar
2 eggs

2 c. all-purpose flour
1 tsp. baking powder
1/2 tsp. baking soda
salt
1 tsp. cinnamon
1/2 tsp. ea nutmeg, ginger, cloves
1/2 cup chocolate chips
1/2 cup chopped walnuts

Preheat oven to 350°. Combine dry ingredients; stir into creamed mixture and blend well. In a separate bowl, cream butter and add sugar, eggs and pumpkin, stirring until well blended, then add to dry ingredients, mixing well. Stir in chocolate chips and nuts. Pour into an oiled and floured lg. loaf pan. Bake for 45-50 minutes or until knife inserted in center comes out clean. Cool on a wire rack.

Glaze Frosting

1-1/2 tbsp. heavy cream
1/2 c. confectioners' sugar

Mix sugar with cream and spoon over top of cake after cake cools.

Pumpkin Spice Muffins

This is one of my favorite muffin recipes. It comes out nice and moist, and you can add raisins and nuts or chocolate chips for more variety. Doesn't get much easier.
1 lg. can pumpkin
1 box spice cake mix
2 eggs

Preheat oven to 350°. Mix the ingredients in a big bowl. Spoon 2/3 full into oiled muffin tins. Bake 15 - 20 minutes, or until toothpick inserted into center comes out clean.

Hearty Pumpkin Banana Nut Muffins

1 lg. can pumpkin
2 ripe bananas
2 eggs
1/2 cup pecans
1/3 cup vegetable oil
1 cup all-purpose flour
1 cup dry quick oatmeal
1/4 cup ground flax flour
1/4 cup cornmeal
1 c. brown sugar
1 tsp cinnamon
1/2 tsp. ea. nutmeg, ground cloves, ginger
1-1/2 tsp baking powder
salt

Preheat oven to 350°. Combine all dry ingredients including spices in a large bowl. Add eggs, oil, pumpkin and bananas, stirring until well blended. Stir in nuts. Oil muffin tins and fill each one 2/3 full. Bake 15 - 20 minutes, or until knife inserted in center comes out clean. Remove from muffin tin and cool on rack. Makes up to 2 dozen muffins.

Pumpkin Sour Cream Muffins

1 lg. can pumpkin
1-1/2 c. all-purpose flour
1 c. sour cream
3 eggs
1/2 c. butter, softened
3/4 c. brown sugar
1 tsp. vanilla
1-1/2 tsp. baking powder
salt
1 tsp. cinnamon
1/2 tsp. ea. allspice, nutmeg, ground cloves, ginger

Combine pumpkin, beaten egg, 1/3 cup sugar and pie spice. Spoon 1/2 of batter into 9x13 baking dish; spread to cover. Sprinkle 1/2 of streusel topping over batter. Carefully spread remaining batter over pumpkin mixture. Sprinkle remaining streusel over top. Bake 325 degrees 50-60 minutes.

Streusel Topping

1 c. brown sugar
1/3 c. butter
2 tsp. cinnamon
1 c. chopped nuts

Cream butter, sugar and vanilla in mixing bowl. Add 3 eggs beating well. Combine flour, baking powder and baking soda. Add dry ingredients to butter mixture alternately with sour cream.

Main Events

American Stew in a Pumpkin

1 medium size pumpkin (10 - 12 pounds), lid cut off (save) and scrape out inside
2 c. ea. yellow squash, halved green beans, thinly sliced carrots, and whole corn kernels
1 c. dry red wine
3 lbs. boned beef shoulder (you can substitute pork if you like) cut in 3/4" cubes
1 lg. onion, diced
1 lg. green pepper, diced
3 tbsp. ea. olive oil and butter
2 c. beef broth
1 can tomato paste
3 cloves garlic, minced
1 bay leaf
1/2 tsp. ea. thyme, sweet basil, and rosemary
salt and pepper

Cook onions and peppers in olive oil and butter in skillet until tender but not browned. Place in a heavy lidded kettle. Brown beef, a few pieces at a time, and add to the kettle. When meat is done, remove from heat, and add onions, peppers, and other vegetables (except pumpkin). Add wine and broth and seasonings and bring to a boil. Turn down heat and continue to simmer for 15 minutes. Place mixture in pumpkin shell, replace lid, and place pumpkin in a shallow baking pan with 1/2" water in the bottom. Bake at 350° in preheated oven for one hour, or until pumpkin and meat are tender when tested with a form. Remove from oven and cool for a few minutes before serving. Serve scoopfuls of the pumpkin, or you can slice it and have a slice available with each serving. This would likely serve 4 - 6 people depending on how much you eat.

Corn and Pumpkin Chowder in the Shell

1 medium pumpkin (10 - 12 pounds), lid cut off and saved, and seeds and membranes removed
4 c. whole kernel corn
1 lg. onion, finely diced
1 lg. green pepper, diced
2 ripe tomatoes, diced
2 stalks celery stalks, diced
3 cloves garlic, minced
4 strips bacon, cooked crisp and crumbled (optional)
3 c. light cream
1 c. bread crumbs
3 tbsp. butter
2 tbsp. olive oil
1 tbsp. sugar
1/2 tsp. cinnamon
1 bay leaf
salt
1 tsp. paprika

Sauté garlic, onion, green pepper and celery in the oil in a large kettle until tender. Add seasonings (except paprika and sugar) and tomato, simmering 10 minutes. Add corn and cream, cooking slowly and stirring frequently until corn is tender. Remove from heat and cool. When cool, pour mixture into pumpkin. Dot with butter and sprinkle sugar and paprika over all. Put pumpkin into a shallow pan with

1/2" water and bake in preheated oven at 300° for 1 hour or until pumpkin meat is tender. Sprinkle top of soup mixture with breadcrumbs and continue to bake at 325° until breadcrumbs are golden brown (15 - 25 minutes). Soup should be served with scoops of the pumpkin and you can sprinkle the crumbled bacon on each serving. This should serve 4 - 6 hungry people and would be good with hot French bread or rolls and a good green salad.

Pumpkin-stuffed Chicken

1 large whole chicken
3 c. cooked, mashed pumpkin
1/2 c. ea. hulled sunflower seeds and chopped pecans, walnuts and raisins
1 c., diced apple (unpeeled)
1 c. chopped celery
salt and pepper

Combine ingredients and lightly stuff into chicken cavity. Bake for 1 hour at 350°, or until chicken is tender and nicely browned. Serves 4 if it isn't the only dish, and if no one asks for seconds. You can also bake your stuffing in an oiled shallow pan for 30 minutes if you prefer. This stuffing would be great with turkey too.

Cajun Pumpkin

1 small pumpkin, 5 - 6 lbs. with top cut off and saved and seeds and membrane removed
2 c. uncooked brown rice
3 c. medium shrimp, cleaned and deveined
2 lg. green peppers, diced

1 lg. onion, diced
1 lg. can stewed tomatoes
2 tbsps. butter
3 cloves garlic, minced
4 tbsps. dried chili powder
1 tsp. ea. oregano, parsley, marjoram and thyme
salt and pepper

Sauté shrimps, green peppers, onion and garlic in the butter. Place rice in bottom of pumpkin and cover with remaining ingredients. Put lid on and place pumpkin in shallow baking pan with 1/2" water. Bake at 350° for 1 hour or until fork inserted in pumpkin comes out clean. Allow to cool 10 - 15 minutes before serving. Scoop out some of the pumpkin with each serving. Serves 4 if no one asks for seconds and if there are other things to go with it. I always figure people want seconds.

Pumpkin Ranchero

4 c. cubed pumpkin
2 lb. cubed pork shoulder
1 lg. green bell pepper, diced
1 - 4 oz. can diced green chilies
1 lg. can stewed tomatoes
2 c. grated Jack cheese
1/2 c. sour cream
1/4 c. sliced green onions
1 can (4 ounces) sliced ripe olives
2 c. string beans, halved
2 c. whole kernel corn
3 cloves garlic, minced
1 can (4 ounces) sliced ripe olives

1/4 c. cooking oil
1 c. water
Salt and pepper
Fresh cilantro

Brown cubed pumpkin in large skillet and then add green pepper and garlic and cook till tender. Put ingredients into large kettle and add remaining ingredients except for fresh cilantro, Jack cheese, sour cream, green onions and ripe olives.

Cover and cook on medium until mixture begins to boil, then turn heat to low and continue to cook until pork and pumpkin are tender when stuck with fork. Turn control to high, stir in cheese and continue stirring until cheese is melted. Place in shallow casserole to serve. Top with sour cream and sprinkle on green onions. Garnish with sliced ripe olives and dollops of sour cream. Serves 4 to 6, depending on how hungry everyone is. I always tend to think on the small size when it comes to how many a recipe will serve because it is embarrassing if they ask for seconds and you have none.

Pipian Empanadas

1/2 c. hulled green pumpkin seeds
3 c. all-purpose flour
1-1/2 c. cornmeal
1/2 lb. ground beef
1 sm. onion, diced
1/4 c. bell pepper, diced
3 cloves garlic, minced
1 medium tomato, chopped

3 potatoes, peeled and diced
2 green onions, chopped
1 hard-boiled egg
1 raw egg (safe for coating empanadas)
1-1/4 c. water
3/4 c. cooking oil
2 tsps. ground cumin
1/4 c. chicken broth
2 tbsps. wine vinegar
3 tbsps. sugar
1-1/2 tsp. baking powder
1/2 tsp. ground cinnamon
salt

Hot Sauce (See recipe below dough and filling)

Dough

Combine flour, cornmeal, sugar, baking powder and salt in a medium bowl. Add oil and work with fingertips until the mixture becomes crumbly. Add water and knead just until dough holds together on its own. Divide the dough into two equal rolls, wrap in plastic and refrigerate for no less than 30 minutes. This recipe does well left overnight before cooking.

Filling

Heat a medium skillet over medium-low heat. Add pumpkin seeds and cook, stirring, until lightly browned. Put seeds into a blender and grind to a fine powder. Cook ground beef in the skillet over medium heat, breaking it up as you would for spaghetti, until it is lightly and thoroughly browned. Drain meat and add onion, bell pepper and garlic; stirring frequently until soft. Stir in tomato, cumin, broth, vinegar, potatoes, salt, and Pipian (ground pumpkin seeds). Reduce heat to medium-low; cover and cook for 10 to 15 minutes. Stir in green onions and hard-boiled egg. Put in large bowl and allow to cool completely in the refrigerator.

Meanwhile, prepare **Hot Sauce** according to the recipe below and set aside.

Hot Sauce

10 green onions, chopped
2 Serrano chilies, seeded and stems removed and chopped fine
2 tbsps. fresh cilantro, stems removed and leaves chopped fine
1/2 c. vinegar
1/4 c. lime juice
1/2 tsp. salt

Combine scallions, chilies, cilantro, vinegar, lime juice and salt to taste in a small bowl and set aside. This is served with the empanadas.

Preheat oven to 350°. Oil two baking sheets. On a well-floured surface, roll out one roll at a time to about 1/8 inch thick. Cut circles of dough using a 4 1/2-inch round cookie cutter, or use a jar lid of approx. size to mark and cut through the dough. You should end up with 24 circles. Beat raw egg and brush the edges of the dough circles. Place about 2 tbsps. filling in the center of each circle. Fold filled circles in half, press edges together and crimp with a fork. Place on the prepared baking sheets. Brush egg glaze over the empanadas. Bake the empanadas until golden and crisp, switching the position of the pans around 25 - 30 minutes. The empanadas should cook 55 to 60 minutes. Let cool for 5 minutes. Serve warm, accompanied by Hot Sauce.

Pumpkin Mole

Meat of one small pumpkin, cubed
2 lbs. shredded beef or one chicken, roasted and shredded
1 lg. can stewed tomatoes
1 med. Onion, diced
3 cloves garlic, minced
2 sprigs fresh cilantro, chopped fine
3 c. whole kernel corn
3 c. pinto beans
8 c. water
1/2 c. mole powder or 1 jar of mole
2 tsp. ground cinnamon
1/2 tsp. nutmeg
1 tsp. ground sage
salt and pepper

Cover meat, seasonings, onions and garlic with water and simmer over medium heat until liquid is reduced by half. Add pumpkin and remaining ingredients and continue to cook for 30 minutes, or until pumpkin is soft when pierced with a fork. Good served with cooked rice.

Pumpkin Mole II

1/4 hulled raw green pumpkin seeds
2 tbsps. peanut butter
1 small onion, diced

1 c. chicken broth
1-1/2 c. tomato sauce
2 cloves garlic, minced
2 tbsp. masa harina
salt
2 tsps. cinnamon
1 tsp. nutmeg

Put all ingredients except chicken broth through blender until smooth. Add pureed mixture to the chicken broth in a saucepan. Bring to boil and reduce heat to simmering for 10 minutes, stirring occasionally to blend. Serve hot. Makes about 2-1/2 c. sauce. Good with chicken, turkey, or seafood cooked in the sauce.

Stuffed Persian Delight

1 medium pumpkin, top cut off and discarded, seeds and membrane removed
2 lbs. boneless lamb, cubed (This is one of the very few lamb recipes I kept in the book. If you don't feel up to using lamb, you could substitute pork or chicken, or you could make it meatless. It will still be quite good.)

1 large onion, diced
3 sweet potatoes, peeled and diced
1 c. ea. apricots and raisins
2 apples, peeled and diced
1 large green pepper, seeded and diced
2 c. beef broth
2 tsps. grated orange peel
1 tsp. ea. cinnamon, ginger
1/2 tsp. ea. ground cloves, nutmeg, cardamom

2 tbsps. butter
1 c. blanched, slivered almond
1/2 c. salt and pepper

Cook meat and onion in large skillet until meat is lightly browned and tender. Add remaining ingredients (except pumpkin), and simmer for 30 minutes. Butter inside of pumpkin and sprinkle lightly with salt. Spoon ingredients into pumpkin shell. Place in shallow baking pan with 1/2" water covering the bottom of the pan. Bake at 325° for one hour, or until pumpkin is tender when tested with a form. Cool slightly and serve with spoonfuls of pumpkin. Serves 4 - 6.

Pumpkin Mexican Style

1 small pumpkin, lid cut and saved, seeded and membranes removed
1 lb. rice, uncooked
1 lg. green bell pepper, seeded and diced
1 sm. onion, diced
3 cloves garlic, minced
2 lbs. medium shrimp
2 tbsps. Butter
salt and pepper
1 c. chicken broth

Clean and devein shrimps. Sauté shrimps, green bell pepper, onion and garlic in butter. Place rice in pumpkin, cover with remaining ingredients. Put lid on pumpkin and place in shallow baking pan with 1/2" water at 325o for 1-1/2 hours or until pumpkin is tender when pierced with fork. To serve, remove lid and scoop out pumpkin-rice-shrimp mixture. Serves 4 - 6.

Basque Pumpkin Stew

Note: This dish is traditionally served on November 1 in the Basque countries.

2 lbs. beef chuck or round
1 med. Pumpkin, lid removed and discarded, seeded and membranes removed
3 sweet potatoes, peeled and cubed
1 lg. green bell pepper, diced
2 lg. tomatoes chopped.
3 white potatoes, peeled and cubed
1 c. dried apricots
1-1/2 c. corn kernels
1 lg. onion, chopped fine
2 c. beef or vegetable broth
1 tbsp. honey
3 tbsps. oil
salt and pepper

Brown meat, onion and garlic in oil in large kettle. Add tomatoes, green bell pepper, seasonings, honey, apricots, white and sweet potatoes and broth (don't add corn yet). Cover and simmer 1 hour. Brush pumpkin inside with butter. Add in ingredients and corn. Place pumpkin in a shallow baking dish with 1/2" water and bake at 325o or until pumpkin and meet are tender. Transfer pumpkin to a large bowl and serve, scooping out pumpkin with each serving. Serves 4 -6.

Caribbean Pumpkin

1 small pumpkin, lid cut and saved, seeded and membranes removed
2 lbs. ground beef
6 oz. Ground smoked ham
2-1/2 c. onion, chopped finely
1 green bell pepper, seeded and chopped
3 lg. cloves garlic, minced
3/4 c. raisins
1/4 c. capers
1/3 c. pimiento-stuffed green olives, sliced
1 can tomato sauce
3 beaten eggs
2 tsp. ea. olive oil, vinegar & oregano
salt and pepper
boiling, salted water - enough to cover pumpkin.

Place pumpkin in large pan and cover with salted boiling water. Cover pan. Bring water to a boil, then simmer until pumpkin meat is almost tender when pierced with a form. The pumpkin should still be able to hold its shape. Remove pumpkin from hot water, drain well and dry the outside. Sprinkle inside with a little salt.

Heat oil in large skillet and add beef, ham, onions, green bell peppers and garlic. Cook over medium heat, stirring constantly until meat is slightly brown and crumbly. Remove from heat and mix remaining spices and garlic. Add to the meat along with the raisins, olives, capers and tomato sauce, mixing well. Cover pan and allow to cook over low heat for 15 minutes, stirring occasionally. Remove from heat and cool slightly, then mix eggs in thoroughly.

Fill cooked pumpkin with meat stuffing, pressing stuffing slightly to pack it firmly. Cover loosely with the pumpkin lid. Place in a shallow greased baking pan and bake at 350⁰ for 45 minutes - 1 hour or until pumpkin is tender. Allow to cool about 10 - 15 minutes before serving. Scoop out pumpkin with other ingredients. Serves 2 - 4.

Mediterranean Stuffed Pumpkin

1 Medium pumpkin, lid cut and saved, seeds and membrane removed
1 lb. ground beef
3 c. cooked rice
4 fresh tomatoes, peeled and chopped
1 medium onion, diced
1 lg. green pepper, seeded and diced
3 cloves garlic, minced
1 tbsp. capers, drained and rinsed
1 c. raisins
1 c. dry white wine
3 tbsps. butter
1/2 c. Parmesan cheese, grated
1/2 tsp. dried thyme and sweet basil
Fresh parsley sprigs
1 bay leaf
salt and pepper

Cut lid from pumpkin and cover pumpkin with water up to just below lid in a large kettle. Cook for 45 minutes or until tender but still holds shape well. In a large skillet, melt butter and sauté onion, green pepper and garlic for 5 minutes. Add beef, pepper and seasonings, cooking over moderate heat while stirring constantly. Add tomatoes, wine and raisins, and simmer until liquid is reduced by half.

Remove from heat, add cooked rice and stuff into pumpkin. Sprinkle with Parmesan cheese and put pumpkin gently into a shallow baking pan. Bake in a 250° oven for 15 minutes, or until cheese is brown. Replace lid on pumpkin before serving. Serve with a ring of parsley springs.

African Pumpkin Stew

1/2 small pumpkin, 4 - 5 lbs.
2 lg. carrots, peeled and diced
1 lg. red onion, coarsely chopped
1 lb. tomatoes, diced
1 c. water
1 tsp. ground coriander
1 tsp. ground cumin
2 tsps. chili powder
1/2 tsp. dried thyme leaves, chopped fine
1/2 tsp. ea. ground cloves and nutmeg
salt and freshly ground black pepper
1 cup roasted, unsalted peanuts, coarsely chopped.

Wash the pumpkin and cut it in half, removing membranes and seeds. Cut the pumpkin into 1-inch cubes, place them in a steamer with adequate water, steaming them until tender but still firm, about 8 to 12 minutes. Set aside.
Put carrots, red onion, tomatoes, water, salt, coriander, cumin, chili powder, thyme, cloves, and pepper in a heavy skillet, and simmer about 30 minutes or until the vegetables are softened. Add steamed pumpkin and half the peanuts, and heat thoroughly for a few more minutes. Transfer to a serving bowl, and sprinkle with the remaining peanuts. This is good served with steamed rice and greens. Serves 2 - 4.

Pumpkin and Cabbage Stew

1 lb. pumpkin, steamed until tender, peeled and cubed
1-1/2 lbs. beef or pork cut into 1" cubes
1/2 lb. cabbage, shredded
4 large green onions, sliced thinly
1 can beef broth
1 tsp. olive oil
3 cubes garlic, minced
salt and pepper

Heat olive oil in a large, deep skillet and sauté meat lightly until thoroughly browned. Transfer into a kettle and add garlic, green onions and seasonings, pumpkin and cabbage, beef broth, and simmer over low heat until cabbage and pumpkin are tender, adding water as needed. Serve hot over cooked rice. Serves 2 – 4, depending on how much you give each person and if it is a main or side dish.

Pumpkin Chili

1 can pumpkin
1 lg. can tomato sauce
1 lg. can kidney beans, drained
1 lg. can diced tomatoes, including liquid
1 can kernel corn
1 sm. can diced green chilies
1 pound ground beef or turkey
1 c. onion, diced
1 ea. red and green bell pepper, diced
2 cloves garlic, minced
2 tbsps. olive oil
1 pkg. chili seasoning
salt and freshly ground black pepper

Heat oil in deep skillet and add crumbled beef or turkey, onion, garlic, green and red bell peppers, and salt and pepper. Sauté until meat is well browned. Transfer to a kettle and add pumpkin, tomato sauce, kidney beans, diced tomatoes with liquid, kernel corn, diced green chilies and bring to boil. Reduce heat and add chili per package instructions. The one I use includes masa, which can be used to thicken the chili. Simmer and stir occasionally for 15 minutes until chili is thoroughly heated.

Serving Suggestion: Serve with grated Cheddar cheese, diced green onion and dollops of sour cream. No decent bowl of the red would be complete without good hot cornbread and red wine or beer. Serves 2 - 4.

Pork and Pumpkin Stew

1 small (4 - 5 lb.) pumpkin, seeds and membranes removed, peeled and cubed
1 lb. lean pork
1 lg. can diced tomatoes
1 med. green bell pepper, seeded and diced
1 med. onion, peeled and chopped fine
2 med. cloves garlic, finely minced
1 sm. can tomato paste
3 tbsps. lemon juice
1 tbsp. dried, crushed mint leaves
salt and pepper

Combine pork, water and seasonings in heavy saucepan. Bring to a boil, removing scum that rises to the top. Reduce heat and add garlic, tomatoes, tomato paste and lemon juice. Cover and simmer for 45 minutes. Stir in pumpkin and bell pepper. Simmer for 15 - 30 min. more or until pumpkin is tender. Serve with cooked rice. Serves 2 - 4.

Pumpkin Tamales

2 c. canned pumpkin
1 1/2 c. masa harina
1 tsp. baking powder
1 tsp. salt
1/4 c. ea. butter and vegetable shortening
3/4 cup warm water
1 c. corn kernels
28 - 30 lg. dried cornhusks, soaked in warm water for 20 min. (14 will be used for the tamales. The rest will be used to provide extra protection during steaming)

Combine the pumpkin, masa harina, baking powder, and salt in a mixing bowl. Add butter and shortening and mix for several minutes, or until thoroughly blended. Add the water and mix until you have a smooth mix. Add the corn kernels and blend thoroughly. Wrap the masa dough in plastic wrap and let it rest at room temperature for 30 minutes.

Filling

1 can black beans
1 sm. onion, minced
3 cloves roasted garlic, chopped
2 tbsps. olive oil
1 tsp. vinegar
1/2 cup cheddar cheese

Sauté onion and garlic in 1/2 tbsp. olive oil in a small pan over medium heat until lightly. Transfer to a blender, add the black beans and vinegar, and purée until smooth. Heat the remaining oil over low heat in a heavy saucepan, add the puréed bean mix and fry, stirring constantly, for 15 to 20 minutes, or until the edges of the purée becomes crusty. Stir in the cheese and cool.

Assembling and Cooking Tamales

You need a large kettle size steamer to cook your tamales. Tear strips of the soaked cornhusks to use for ties. There are several ways to close the cornhusks once you have stuffed the tamale recipe into them. You can simply fold them over like a little package, and you can tie around the package if you like. Or you can stuff them in the middle and then roll the cornhusks and tie them on both ends. And finally, if you like, you can roll the cornhusks and fold them over and tie them with just one tie at the top.

To stuff the cornhusks, spread about 3 lg. tbsps. of the masa mix over the smooth side of the cornhusks. Where you spread it depends on which tying method you will use. For the folded method, you need to spread it in the top half of the cornhusks. For the double tie method, you need to spread it in the middle part of the cornhusk, and for the single tie method, spread it as you would for the double tied method. Instead of folding it like a package, you will fold it over in half and then roll the cornhusk and tie the part that is loose at one end. Just think of how you would make a little hobo sack and that will make it an easy method. All three methods are actually simple. The double tying just takes a little longer, and the little folded method is probably the fastest.

Once you have spread your masa on your cornhusk, make a little indention and put a tbsp. or a little more on the filling, spreading it evenly.

When you have all your cornhusks bundled up and ready to go, put them into the steamer with an appropriate amount of water (it will fill the bottom area UNDER the cornhusks, but should not cover them). As you begin to put them in, put in some extra cornhusks and then start putting in your tamales. If you need to layer your tamales (you can stand them on end if they are double or single tied, and lay them down if they are folded), put some extra cornhusks between the layers before adding more tamales.

Make sure there are cornhusks all around the outside edges of the tamales and on top too. The cornhusks keep your tamales dry inside if you have to add additional water. Cooking tamales is sort of an intuitive, mystical process. You put on your lid (after you have your water and tamales inside), and turn on the heat and wait. Meanwhile you pour yourself a nice glass of wine or you can have a coffee or tea, whatever you usually drink. In about 30 minutes, you want to start testing your tamales. Get a pair of tongs and take out one tamale. Unwrap the tamale and if the masa is still sticking to the cornhusk, it is not done yet. You don't have to worry about the filling. It is already cooked. Rewrap your tamale and put it back with the others. Check again in another 5 - 10 minutes and it will probably be done.

Because of the time involved with making tamales, be sure to give yourself plenty of time. This is not a quick and easy dinner. In fact, lots of folks make their tamales way ahead of time, freeze them, defrost them when needed and then microwave them a minute or two, (do no more than a couple at a time for best results). You can also used cooked, shredded chicken or beef for your filling, or if you are very adventuresome, make a sweet filling (like a pumpkin pie filling) with nuts and raisins and other favorite dried fruits. It will make a delicious desert tamale.

Prospector's Pumpkin

This very old recipe came from an elderly friend who had lived in South Africa for many years and who remembered preparing it. It was originally cooked over wood stoves and was a favorite among South Africans. Pumpkins or other hard-shelled squashes there are referred to as groundnuts.

2 lbs. lamb or mutton ribs (If you have difficulty getting lamb or mutton, or you just don't want to eat it, you can use pork or chicken
1 small (4 - 5 lbs.) pumpkin, seeds and membranes removed, peeled and cubed
3 thinly sliced medium onions
1 small can of dry chili
1/4 c. chutney
2 tbsps. olive oil
Salt and pepper

Trim the meat from the ribs and put into a deep skillet in the olive oil. Add the sliced onions and sauté until meat is browned and onions translucent. Add pumpkin to meat, mixing thoroughly. Add chopped green chili and chutney and cook until tender, adding a little more oil only if needed. Serve with cooked rice.

Pig-in-a-Pumpkin

1 small pumpkin (4 - 5 pounds) with lid, seeds and membranes removed and discarded
1 lb. pork sausage
1 slightly beaten egg
1 c. chopped celery
1/2 c. sliced fresh mushrooms
1/2 c. diced onion
1/2 c. sour cream
1/4 c. grated Parmesan cheese
salt and pepper

Lightly salt the inside of the pumpkin and stuff it with a mixture of ingredients. Place open side of pumpkin face down in shallow oiled baking dish and bake at 350° until tender - 45 min. - 1 hr.

Pumpkin Rarebit

2 c. mashed, cooked pumpkin or 1 lg. can
1/2 c. ea. grated Gruyere and Parmesan cheese
2 c. white sauce (recipe below)
1 c. water
1 tsp. ea. parsley, sweet basil and paprika
2 tbsps. butter
salt and pepper
Toasted whole wheat bread (2 slices per person - recipe serves 4 unless someone is very hungry.)

White Sauce

2 c. milk
4 tbsps. butter
4 tbsps. flour

To make white sauce, melt 4 tbsps. butter and stir in flour slowly, using a wire whisk to help keep it smooth. Add milk a little at a time, continuing to stir with the whisk. Stir pumpkin and seasonings into the sauce. Put mixture into an oiled casserole and sprinkle with cheese. Dot with more butter and bake in 350° oven for 25 - 30 minutes, or until cheese is melted and slightly browned. Serve over whole wheat toast. This is a good light supper on a cold evening, served with hot tea and perhaps a light green salad.

Pumpkin-Cashew Cutlets

1 lg. can pumpkin or 2 c. cooked, mashed
1/2 lb. cashews, unsalted and chopped finely
1 med. onion, diced
1 med. bell pepper, seeded and diced
2 c. green peas
2 med. carrots, peeled and diced
1/4 lb. grated cheddar or white cheese
1 tsp. dried parsley
1/2 tsp. powdered sage
salt
2 tbsps. oil

Steam all vegetables except pumpkin until tender. Meanwhile, sauté onion in oil over low heat until slightly golden. Mix onion and vegetables and mash together. Mix in eggs, cheese, pumpkin and cashew pieces. Form mixture into 8 cutlets or patties if you are not sure what a cutlet looks like. Place on oiled baking sheet in 350° oven for about 15 min. Reduce heat to 300° and bake for another 15 minutes, or until knife inserted comes out clean. Serves 2 - 4.

Pumpkin Polenta

1 lg. can pumpkin
1 cu. chopped onion
1 sm. can chopped jalapeños
1 can enchilada sauce
3 small cloves garlic, minced
3/4 tsp. ground cinnamon
salt and pepper
Polenta (see recipe below)
1 tbsp. olive oil
1 c. shredded cheddar cheese

Put olive oil in bottom of kettle. Add onions and sauté until slightly brown. Add jalapeno, cinnamon and garlic and continue to stir. Add a small amount of water to prevent sticking if necessary. Stir in enchilada sauce, cover and simmer 5 minutes. Add mashed pumpkin, salt and pepper and stir well. Simmer uncovered 3 additional minutes, stirring continuously. Remove from heat.

Prepare basic polenta recipe and spread half of it in 11 x 7 x 2 inch oiled baking dish. Spread pumpkin mixture evenly over polenta. Sprinkle with cheese and spread remaining polenta evenly over everything. Bake at 375° for 30 minutes or until lightly browned. Let stand 5 minutes before serving. Serves 4 with some other dishes as sides. Black beans and a salad would be nice accompaniments.

Basic Polenta

1 1/4 cups cornmeal
4 cups water
salt

Place cornmeal and salt in large saucepan. Gradually add water, stirring constantly with a wire whisk. Bring to a boil, reduce heat to medium, and uncovered 15 minutes, stirring frequently. Remove from heat and cool slightly before spreading in oiled baking pan.

Pumpkin Lasagna

1 lg. can pumpkin
1 c. sliced mushrooms
3 c. mozzarella cheese, grated
1/2 cup Parmesan cheese, grated
1 1/4 cup sour cream
1 med. onion, diced
2 cloves garlic, minced
2 tbsps. vegetable or olive oil
2 tbsps. dried sage, crumbled
2 tbsps. green onions, freshly chopped
salt and freshly cracked black pepper
1 pkg. lasagna noodles, cooked according to package instructions

Sauté the thinly sliced onion and garlic in the oil until lightly browned. Mix together the pumpkin, onion and garlic mix, mushrooms and seasonings.

Lightly oil an 11 x 7 x 2 baking dish. Place a layer of lasagna in bottom of dish, top with a third of the pumpkin mixture then a third of the combined cheeses. Repeat with the remaining lasagna, pumpkin and cheeses.

Mix the sour cream with the green onions, and spread over the top of the dish. Bake at 350° for 35-40 minutes until slightly browned on edges. Serves 2 - 4. This is good with a mixed green salad and some red wine.

Down Under Pumpkin Veggie Pie

3 c. lightly steamed, cubed, peeled pumpkin
1 c. green peas
1 c. raw zucchini, sliced
2 tsps. vegetable seasoning
1 tsp. ground pepper
1 pie crust with 1/4 c. sesame seeds mixed in (use prepared pie crust mix or make your favorite pie crust recipe and add the sesame seeds)

Steam the vegetables. Mash the mixture and spread over the bottom crust in a medium pie plate. Add top crust and cut vents, and you can add a pumpkin shape cut from the crust mix to the top crust. Bake at 425° or until crust is golden brown. Serves 4 - 6. Note: For variety, you can add other steamed vegetables (1 c. each will do) such as carrots, cauliflower or corn kernels. You can also add some grated mild cheddar cheese under the top crust for a delicious dish. This is good with a light salad.

Pumpkin Ravioli

1 can canned pumpkin
1 cup ricotta cheese
2 lg. eggs
2 c. flour
1 sm. can tomato paste
1 tbsp. vegetable or olive oil
salt
1/2 tsp. nutmeg

Mix the cheese, pumpkin, salt and nutmeg and set aside.

Mix flour, and 1 tsp. salt in a large bowl. Make an indentation in the center of the flour. Beat the eggs, tomato paste and oil until well blended and pour into the center of the flour. Stir with a fork and until the dough makes a ball. If the dough is too dry, add up to 2 tbsps. of water. Knead lightly on a floured cloth-covered surface until smooth and elastic, about 5 minutes. You can add a little flour if the dough is too sticky as you knead it. Cover and let rest for another 5 minutes.

Divide dough into 4 equal parts. Roll dough, one part at a time, into a rectangle about 12 X 10-inches. (Keep the remaining dough covered while you are rolling the other parts.)

Place 2 level tsps. in 2 rows of 4 mounds each 1 1/2-inches apart on the dough rectangle. Moisten the outer edges of the dough and the dough between the rows of pumpkin mixture with water. Fold the other half of the dough up over the pumpkin mixture, pressing the dough down around the pumpkin, trimming the edges with a knife. Cut between the rows of filling to make the ravioli. Press the edges together with a fork. Repeat this process with the remaining dough and pumpkin filling. Place ravioli on paper towel, and pat outside dry on both sides.

Cook ravioli in a large saucepan in 4 quarts of boiling salted water until tender, about 10 to 15 minutes; drain carefully. While ravioli is cooking, prepare pumpkinseed sauce (see below). This is about right for two people and I would serve with a nice green salad and perhaps some good thick slices of French bread.

Pumpkin Sauce for Raviolis

1 sm. can pumpkin
1 sm. onion, diced
1 med. green bell pepper, diced
2 lg. cloves garlic, minced
2 tbsps. butter
1 c. chicken broth
1/4 c. heavy cream
1/4 c. water
4 tbsps. fresh parsley, chopped fine
1 tsp. nutmeg

In a large deep skillet, sauté the onion, bell pepper, and garlic in butter until softened. Stir in remaining ingredients and simmer, stirring occasionally, for 10 minutes. Serve over ravioli.

Stuffed Pumpkin

One of my favorite dishes my mom made was bell peppers stuffed with a sort of meatloaf and rice mixture and tomato sauce. I have made my own version using miniature pumpkins I had and didn't want to throw away when Halloween was over.

4 small green pumpkins
2 c. cooked white rice
2 lb. of ground beef or turkey
1 small can diced stewed tomatoes
1 1/2 tsps. dried basil)
1/2 tsp. dry savory or thyme
1/2 tsp. ground marjoram
1/4 cup olive oil
Salt and pepper
Paprika

Cut the tops off of the pumpkins. Remove and discard the tops, the inner strings and seeds. Place pumpkins cut side up on a steaming rack over water almost up to rack in a large covered pot. Bring to boil and steam for 10 minutes or until somewhat soft as you would do a bell pepper. You can omit this step of steaming if you like and just have them as baked in the oven.

Mix the filling: Heat oven to 350°F. In a large bowl mix together the ground beef, seasonings (except the paprika) and cooked rice. Mix in the stewed tomatoes.

Remove pumpkins from steamer pan. Place cut side up in a Pyrex or other casserole to fit. Gently stuff the pumpkins with the ground beef rice mixture.

Drizzle olive oil over the stuffed pumpkins, along the outside of them, and into the pan. Rub the oil over the outside of the pumpkins. Sprinkle the tops generously with paprika.

Place on the middle rack of the oven and bake at 350°F for 35 minutes, or until the meat mixture is cooked. Sprinkle the paprika over the pumpkin top and perhaps put a sprig of parsley on top for a nice look. Serve with hot bread of your choice.

Asides

Pumpkin with Cornmeal

1 can pumpkin
1 c. cornmeal
1/4 c. peanut butter
2 c. water
1/4 c. sugar
salt

Bring water to a boil in a large saucepan and add the corn meal. Cook, stirring frequently, until it thickens. Stir in the mashed pumpkin, then add the sugar, peanut butter and salt. Continue to cook for a few minutes over low heat, adding about ½ cup water if it becomes too dry. This dish is popular in some parts of Africa. Serves 2 - 4.

Pumpkin Blossoms Mediterranean

3 dozen pumpkin blossoms
1 can stewed tomatoes, drained
1 c. brown rice, uncooked
1 sm. can chopped ripe olives
4 green onions, chopped
2 cloves garlic, minced
2 tbsps. fresh parsley, chopped
2 tbsps. fresh mint, chopped
3 tbsps. olive oil
Juice of 1 lemon
1 tbsp. sugar
salt and pepper

Gather blossoms early in the morning and soak the stems in cold water until ready to use. Just before using, wash and drain blossoms on a paper towel. Cut off stems and discard. Set blossoms aside while you make filling. Note: If you do not have your own blossoms, you can generally find some squash or pumpkin blossoms (either will work) through the summer and into the early autumn at your local farmers market.

Sauté the green onions in the oil until soft. Add the garlic and rice; cook over moderate heat for 2 minutes, stirring constantly. Stir in tomatoes, herbs, ripe olives and enough water to cover rice; add salt, pepper and sugar. Simmer for 5 minutes. Stuff each blossom carefully with approximately 1 tsp. of filling. Close the blossoms and lay on their sides in an oiled and lidded flameproof casserole.

Pour 1 c. of warm water over the blossoms, cover the casserole with the lid, and simmer approx. 40 min., or until all water is absorbed. Serve with fresh parsley sprigs for garnish and lemon juice.

Pumpkin Blossom Scramble

4 eggs
2 tbsps. milk
1 dozen pumpkin blossoms
salt and pepper

Beat eggs, milk and seasonings with wire whisk until frothy. Reserve four of the prettiest blossoms. Remove the sepals, stamens and any green from the remaining blossoms and chop finely. Add to eggs and turn into skillet with melted butter. Cook and scramble to desired degree of doneness. Serve with the pumpkin blossoms as a garnish. This will serve 2 people depending on how many eggs you want to eat and also what else you are serving with it. Hot breakfast bread with some good jams would be a good addition.

Pumpkin Tips

Gather the tips, new leaves and stalks of the vines, cutting them quite small. My friend who lived for many years in South Africa told me that South Africans like to include some tiny green pumpkins as well. Cut the pumpkins in half and cook everything in enough water to cover, simmering until tender. For variety, add a few small red chopped potatoes and one small sliced onion. Drain the vegetables when tender, add butter and mash, or serve whole. You might want to grow some vines just for this purpose, though pumpkin vines take a good amount of space.

African Pumpkin Leaves with Peanuts

A good friend who encouraged and helped me a lot with this cookbook originally gave me this recipe from her husband, who grew up in Africa.

3 c. young pumpkin leaves, shredded
2 tomatoes, finely chopped
1 c. roasted peanuts, finely chopped
1/2 c. peanut oil or vegetable oil
1 tsp. cayenne pepper
salt and pepper

Wash leaves thoroughly, removing any tough stems. Put in a pan of boiling, salted water and cook, uncovered, until the leaves are tender. Drain and set aside. Heat oil in a frying pan; add chopped onion and tomatoes, sautéing until onions are tender and slightly golden. Add seasonings and chopped peanuts and cook for a few minutes, stirring constantly. Add leaves; cook about 5 minutes longer, continuing to stir constantly. Serves 2 - 4.

Polish Sour Pumpkin

2 lbs. pumpkin, peeled and cubed
1 c. sour cream
1 tbsp. butter mixed with 1 tbsp. flour
1 c. dill pickle liquid
1 tbsp. ea. fresh dill and parsley, chopped
Salt and pepper

Steam pumpkin until tender, then add remaining ingredients, simmering for 25 minutes, or until tender. Serves 4 - 6.

Tacos al Flor de Calabasa (Pumpkin Blossom Tacos)

The Aztecs used the blossoms of various fruits and vegetables to prepare delicately flavored dishes. Today, many Mexican families in the interior still use the blossoms in a variety of dishes.

4 dozen pumpkin blossoms
20 tortillas

3 large green chilies, washed, deveined and sliced (Be careful to wash your hands and don't touch your face or eyes while you are working with these peppers).
1 c. corn kernels
1 c. green tomatoes, diced
1 med. onion, diced
1-1/2 c. grated cheese
1 c. heavy cream
1 c. oil
1/2 c. fresh cilantro, chopped
salt

Gather flowers early in the morning, wash them and remove stalks and pistils. Put them into ice water until ready to use, then cut petals finely. Sauté onion in 2 tbsps. oil until golden brown. Add chilies, corn and green tomato and cook 6 - 9 min. over slightly reduced heat until soft. Add flowers, seasonings and cilantro and cook for approx. 5 min. more.

Pour remaining oil into a frying pan, heat it and fry the tortillas until they are still soft but beginning to turn golden. Remove and drain them, then spread the flower mixture, roll them up and place them in a baking dish. Cover with cream and sprinkle grated cheese over the top. Put them into the oven and bake for 10 - 15 min. at 350° or until cheese turns brown.

Pumpkin-Soy Bean Loaf

1 lb. steamed, mashed pumpkin or 1 lg. can
1 lb. zucchini, steamed
2 stalks celery, chopped fine

1/2 c. wheat germ
2 c. soy beans, steamed
1 med. onion, diced
2 fresh eggs, beaten
salt

Sauté onion in 2 tbsps. oil until golden. Mix all ingredients and place in oiled loaf pan. Place pan in 350° oven for 30 min., or until knife inserted comes out clean. Allow to cool a few minutes before serving. You can also change this recipe by adding 1/2 c. sliced mushrooms and 1 sm. can tomato paste.

Pumpkin Pudding Parmesan

2 c. mashed pumpkin
3 egg yolks
3 tbsps. grated parmesan cheese
1 c. milk
2 tbsps. flour
1/4 c. + 2 tbsps. butter
Leaves from several sprigs of parsley
salt and pepper

Place pumpkin and 2 tbsps. butter in saucepan and cook gently until pumpkin is dry. Cool and add salt and pepper. In a separate pan, melt 1/4 c. butter, blend in flour and cook over med. heat one minute, stirring constantly. Add milk, blending thoroughly. Continue to cook until mixture thickens. Add sauce to pumpkin and mix well. Stir in egg yolks, one at a time, mixing well after each addition. Add the cheese and place the mixture in a greased mold. Place mold in shallow pan of hot water and cook in over at 350°

for 45 minutes, or until pudding is firm. Turn out onto serving dish and garnish with parsley. Serves 3 - 4.

Incan Pumpkin

1 small pumpkin, (approx. 5 lbs.), lid cut off, membranes and seeds removed, peeled and cubed
1 lg. can tomatoes
1 onion, sliced thinly
1 c. dried bread crumbs
2 tbsps. Tabasco
Salt
1 tsp. ea. powdered ginger and cloves

Put pumpkin cubes into boiling salted water to cover and cook until tender, about 10 - 15 minutes. Remove from heat and drain. In an oiled 2-quart casserole, put in bread crumbs and alternate slices of onion with slices of pumpkin on top. Mix cloves and Tabasco with tomatoes and pour over pumpkin. Dot with butter and bake in a 350° oven for 30 minutes. Serves 4 - 6.

Corn Meal Mush with Pumpkin

4 c. pureed fresh pumpkin or canned pumpkin
2 c. corn meal
4 c. light cream
1 sm. onion, diced
1/2 tsp. ea. crushed rosemary, sage, parsley and sweet basil
1/2 c. butter
salt

Combine pumpkin, cream, corn meal and seasonings, mixing well. Sauté onion in butter until golden brown; add to the mixture. Place in an oiled casserole and bake in a 325° oven for 1 hour, or until knife inserted in center comes out clean.

Baked Pumpkin Patties

2-1/2 c. cooked, mashed fresh pumpkin or canned pumpkin
2 c. cracker crumbs (or dried bread crumbs)
1 c. chopped peanuts
2 eggs
4 tbsps. flour
2 tbsps. butter
salt and pepper
1 tbsp. chopped parsley

Combine pumpkin, peanuts, butter, seasonings, 2 eggs and 2 tbsps. flour. Form into little patties and dip into a batter of 2 eggs and breadcrumbs. Put in 350° oven for 20 minutes, or until crisp outside. Serve with the sauce.

Sauce for Baked Pumpkin Patties

1-1/2 c. light cream
1/2 c. chopped peanuts
2 tbsps. lemon juice
2 tbsps. butter

Mix butter and flour over low heat, adding light cream gradually and stirring with a wire whisk until smooth. Add chopped peanuts and lemon juice, pouring the sauce over the cakes. Serves 2 - 4.

Pumpkin in Coconut Milk

1 very small pumpkin (approx. 2 pounds), lid cut off,
    membranes and seeds removed, peeled and diced
2 cans coconut milk
1/2 tsp. ea. ground cinnamon and cardamon seeds
1-1/2 c. sugar

Put pumpkin and coconut milk into large saucepan, adding seasonings and sugar. Put on stove and bring to a boil. When the mixture is boiling, turn heat down and allow to simmer. When pumpkin is thoroughly tender, remove from heat (Pumpkin will be somewhat dry when ready). Mash with fork and add some butter to top. This is good with pork or chicken. Serves 2 - 4.

Armenian Glazed Pumpkin

1 small pumpkin (approx. 5 lbs.), lid cut off, membranes
    and seeds removed, peeled and cubed
1 c. water
1 c. sugar
2 tbsps. lemon juice
1/4 c. toasted almonds
1 sm. piece gingerroot, peeled and halved
salt

In a heavy saucepan or casserole, bring water to a boil. Add sugar and gingerroot, stirring until sugar dissolves. Add pumpkin and salt and cook over moderate heat until tender and well glazed, adding more water if necessary. Remove gingerroot and discard. Add lemon juice and garnish with almonds. Very good with turkey or pork. Serves 2 - 4.

Curried Pumpkin

2 c. fresh pumpkin, peeled, seeded and cubed
1/2 coconut, grated
2. c. lentils, soaked
1/2 c. yogurt
1 tbsp. vegetable oil
3 tbsps. ground or dried mustard
1 tsp. curry powder

Grind coconut and mustard to a smooth paste in blender. Add yogurt. Heat vegetable oil in large skillet. Add curry and lentils, frying until lentils are crisp. Place pumpkin in serving bowl and stir in other ingredients. Serves 2 - 4. You can vary this recipe by adding 1 tsp. chili powder and 1 tsp. ground cumin seed. Substitute lima beans for the lentils and add 1/4 c. chopped green pepper and 1 sm. chopped onion.

Pigs n' Pumpkin

1 small pumpkin (4 - 5 lbs.), peeled, membranes and seeds removed, and cut into 1" thick slices
8 slices bacon
1/4 cup olive oil
1/4 cup balsamic vinegar
salt and pepper

Preheat charcoal grill to medium heat. Brush pumpkin pieces with olive oil. Season with salt and pepper. Wrap with bacon and place onto grill. Cook for approx. 15 minutes, turning occasionally.

When pumpkin is tender and bacon is crisp, remove from heat and drizzle with balsamic vinegar before serving. Serves 2 - 4.

Pumpkin Omelet

2 c. pureed pumpkin
4 eggs
1/2 c. light cream
3 tbsps. butter or margarine
Salt and pepper

Beat eggs until golden yellow throughout. Mix ingredients, folding eggs in last. Cook over low heat in buttered pan. Fold over and serve on a heated dish when done. Crumbled bacon spread on the top makes a nice variation of this dish.

Pumpkin and Rice Casserole

4 c. pumpkin, cubed and peeled
1 c. brown rice
2 small onions, sliced thin
2 c. turkey or chicken stock
3 tbsps. butter
1/2 tsp. ea. cinnamon, ginger and nutmeg
Salt and pepper

Sauté onion in butter. Add rice, stirring constantly in medium heat until the rice is a crispy golden brown. Remove from heat and add seasoned stock and pumpkin cubes. Cook until pumpkin is tender when pierced with a form, then turn into an oiled casserole and add remaining ingredients. Cook at 350° for 30 minutes. Serves 2 - 4.

This can be varied by serving with a cheese sauce with chopped green bell pepper in it. For another variation, add 1/2 c. ea. raisins, blanched almonds and brown sugar. Omit turkey stock, substituting 2 c. light cream.

Pumpkin and Onion Casserole

1 small pumpkin, cubed, peeled, seeds and membranes removed and boiled until tender, or 1 lg. can pureed pumpkin
3 small onions, minced
3 tbsps. bacon drippings or butter or margarine
1 tsps. ea. fresh minced parsley and basil
Salt and pepper

Preheat oven to 375°. Stir-fry onions in drippings, butter or margarine over moderate heat 3 - 5 minutes or until golden brown. Layer pumpkin and onion (including the drippings or the butter or margarine) in an ungreased 1-1/2 qt. Casserole, seasoning with salt, pepper and herbs. Cover and bake for one hour. Serves 4 - 6. You can also boil the pumpkin, onions and seasonings and then drain them and fry them until they are somewhat crisp (or if you are using pureed pumpkin, fry until it is somewhat solid like a pancake). You need to stir or turn the pumpkin as it is frying. Add 1 c. cooked green peas for a different treat.

New England Baked Pumpkin

1 small pumpkin
5 - 7 tbsps. butter as required to dot cut pumpkin with butter for baking
1/2 c. orange juice
1/2 tsp. ea. cinnamon, nutmeg, ginger, allspice

Cut open a small pumpkin, remove seeds and membranes and cube, but do not peel. Dot heavily with butter, sprinkle with orange juice seasonings all over and place on a baking sheet covered with foil. Bake 1 hour at 375° or until tender when you pierce pumpkin with a fork. Serve with a main dish as you would a baked potato.

Herbed Steamed Pumpkin

4 c. uncooked, cubed pumpkin
1/4 c. chicken stock
1 sm. onion, sliced thinly
1 tsp. ea. ground fresh rosemary, basil, thyme, sage.

Place pumpkin and onion in a steamer and cook until pumpkin is tender. If you don't have a steamer, you can cover it and cook it in water as you would any other fresh vegetable you wanted to cook until tender. If you use the second method, drain pumpkin when it is tender. Add the seasonings and pour heated stock over the pumpkin before serving. Serves 2 - 4.

Pumpkin Carrot Stew

1 sm. pumpkin, peeled, seeded with membranes removed, and cubed (or 1 lg. can pureed pumpkin)
4 lg. carrots, sliced thinly
1 c. prunes, pitted and chopped finely
1/4 c. honey
1/2 tsp. ea. cardamon and nutmeg
Salt and pepper to taste

Put pumpkin and carrots into a pan with just enough water to cover and bring to a boil. Lower heat to simmering and continue to cook until tender. Drain and mash and then set aside. Cover prunes with 1 -1/2 c. or enough to cover. Bring to boil, lower heat and continue to cook until prunes are very tender. Drain liquid and reserve 1 c. of liquid. Add prunes to the pumpkin mixture, and then add the liquid, honey and seasonings. Place in oiled casserole dish and bake at 350° for 15 minutes. Serves 2 - 4 depending on whether people ask for seconds or not.

Deep-fried Pumpkin and Peanuts

1 lg. can pumpkin
1/2 c. peanut butter
1 c. brown rice flower
1/2 c. whole peanuts, shelled
Oil for deep-frying (if this is a health issue for you, you can bake the pumpkin balls you will create at 375° about 20 minutes or until crisp).

If you are frying the pumpkin, pour 3" (approx.) into heavy skillet or deep fryer and heat to 350° F.

Combine pumpkin, peanut butter and salt, blending until smooth and forming 1" diameter balls. Put 1 peanut into each ball. Drop balls into hot oil and deep fry for 1 - 3 minutes, or until crisp. Drain on absorbent paper before serving.

Green Pumpkin Stew

1 med. green (unripe) pumpkin, peeled, seeded and membranes removed, and cubed
2 cups corn kernels
1 med. onion, chopped
2 lg. tomatoes, diced
2 roasted green chilies, peeled, seeded and cubed
2 tbsps. butter or cooking oil
1/2 tsp. garlic powder
Salt and pepper to taste

In a large, deep pot, melt butter or heat cooking oil. Add corn, pumpkin and onion, stirring frequently and cooking slowly until the onion is translucent and the pumpkin soft. Add remaining ingredients and just enough water to cover and prevent sticking. Cover and simmer slowly for 20 more minutes or just until everything is tender and hot. Serve with hot French or garlic bread. Serves 2 - 4.

Jeweled Pumpkin Ring

2 c. pureed pumpkin (1 lg. can)
2 c. fresh peas, shelled (or 1 small package, frozen)
1/2 medium onion, minced
3 eggs, well-beaten (or use the equivalent of egg substitute)
1/2 c. heavy or low fat cream (not whipping cream)
1/4 c. margarine, softened
1/2 c. bread crumbs
Salt and pepper
Mayonnaise

Preheat oven to 350°. Steam fresh peas about 5 minutes, or until tender (You do not need to do this with frozen peas. Just defrost them.) Combine pumpkin, peas, onion, cream, eggs, butter, breadcrumbs and seasonings, mixing well. Pour into a greased one quart ring mold and set in a pan of water that has reached the boiling point. If you don't have the ring mold, you could use a Pyrex type round bowl as long as it will set fit into the water. Put the whole thing into a baking pan and bake 30 minutes, or until the pumpkin is set when tested with a toothpick. Remove from the oven and allow to cool slightly. Turn out onto a plate and add lettuce and/or fresh parsley leaves around it. Serve with spoonfuls of mayonnaise. Serves 2 – 4 depending on size of serving and whether anyone asks for seconds.

Pumpkin Peel Tempura

Peel from 1 medium pumpkin
Oil for deep frying
1/2 c. unbleached flour
1/4 c. water

Cut the peel into thin strips. Make a batter of the flour, water and salt and dip the pumpkin peel until all of it is coated. Pour 3" of oil into a heavy skillet and heat until the oil is bubbling. Spoon the batter-covered strips into the hot oil and deep-fry until golden and crisp. Drain on absorbent paper. If this way of cooking is a health issue for you, you could bake the coated peel in the oven at 350° about 10 - 12 minutes or until it is golden brown and crispy. Can be served with soy sauce, or if you have a sweet tooth, sprinkle with sugar and cinnamon. This is a good side dish with roasted chicken, pork or beef.

Pumpkin Roll

1/2 c. pumpkin puree
1/2 c. sweet potato puree
1-1/2 c. whole wheat flour
1/2 c. rice flour
1 egg yolk, well beaten
2 tbsps. corn oil
1/4 c. water
1 tsp. cinnamon
1/2 tsp. ea. nutmeg, cloves, ginger
salt

Blend the pumpkin and sweet potato purees and season with salt and set aside. Combine flour and seasonings in a large bowl, mixing well. Add oil, rubbing mixture between your palms to blend evenly. Add water gradually to form an elastic dough. Knead for 8 - 10 minutes or until smooth. Form dough into a ball, wrap in a damp cloth and set aside in a refrigerator for 30 minutes.

Divide dough into 2 parts and roll each part on a floured board into a thin rectangular sheet. Spread the purees over the surface of both sheets and roll into cylinders, sealing edges with a few drops of water. Rush tops of rolls with beaten egg yolk and place rolls on a lightly oiled baking pan. Bake in a preheated 350° oven for 25 - 30 minutes, or until nicely browned. Cool slightly before slicing.

Whole Pumpkin Tempura

3 c. sliced, pared pumpkin cut into narrow 3" long strips
1 c. all-purpose flour
1 egg, slightly beaten
1/4 c. sugar
Cooking oil - enough to cover and deep fry the pumpkin strips
1 c. ice water
salt and pepper

Combine flour, sugar, seasoning, ice water, egg and cooking oil and beat until flour is well moistened. Stir in 1 - 2 ice cubes. They don't need to melt before you use the batter. Dip the pumpkin slices into the cold batter. Heat the cooking oil until it reaches 375°. Fry the tempura pieces a few at a time until they are a nice golden brown.

You can also save the peel and treat it the same way separately (see recipe above). Some people might enjoy having the pumpkin cooked with the peel on it as well. I always figure one cup of any main ingredient to a person, so since this has three cups of pumpkin strips, I think three servings might make sense. You could add some mushrooms and some green peppers (you would need to at least double your recipe for the batter), but it would be delicious with shrimp or chicken.

East Indian Pumpkin

2 c. pumpkin, cubed and pared
1 c. lima or butter beans
1/2 c. chopped green bell pepper
1 small onion, sliced thinly

1 c. coconut milk
3 tbsps. butter
1 tsp. cumin powder
1 tsp. chili powder
salt and pepper

Combine vegetables and add enough water in a saucepan to cover. Simmer until tender. Add coconut milk and seasonings and bring to a boil. Lower the heat and continue to simmer until the vegetables are tender when pierced with a fork. Remove from heat and add butter before serving. Serves 2 comfortably.

Pumpkin and Lentil Curry

2 c. cubed pumpkin, pared and steamed
1/2 coconut, grated
1/2 c. lentils, soaked until tender
1/2 c. yogurt
3 tsp. ground mustard
1 tsp. curry powder
2 tbsps. vegetable oil.

Put coconut and mustard in a blender and grind until smooth. Add to yogurt. Heat vegetable oil in a large skillet and add curry and lentils, frying until lentils are crisp. Place pumpkins in a large bowl and add coconut mixture. Blend in the lentils and curry mixture. Comfortably serves 2.

East Indian Gingered Pumpkin

2 c. cubed, peeled pumpkin
2 med. tomatoes, diced
1 sm. onion, finely diced
2 cloves crushed garlic.
1/2 coconut, grated
1 tsp. crushed red dried peppers
1/2 tap. mustard seeds
1/2 tsp. ea. ground turmeric and coriander
2 crushed bay leaves
2 tsps. finely chopped candied ginger

Heat oil in large skillet and add onion and all seasonings except ginger, sautéing for five minutes. Add pumpkin and tomatoes and simmer until pumpkin is tender. Stir in yogurt and coconut and garnish with candied ginger.

Pumpkin Baked in Cinnamon and Cream

Medium sized pumpkin, split in half and seeds and membrane removed
2 pints heavy cream
2 tsps. cinnamon
salt and pepper

Split pumpkin and scoop out seeds. Peel and slice thinly. Oil a medium-size casserole; add a layer of pumpkin and sprinkle with cinnamon, salt and pepper and cream. Repeat until all pumpkin and cream is used. Dot with butter and bake for approximately 1 hour, or until cream is absorbed and pumpkin is tender. Serves between 2 - 4. This is very good served with a pork roast or ham.

Corn and Pumpkin Stew

Corn kernels from 4 ears of corn
1 medium green (unripe) pumpkin
6 chilies anchos, seeded and peeled
2 c. pinto beans, soaked overnight
1 small ham hock or other soup bone
1 tbsp. cilantro, chopped fine
1 tsp. ea. oregano and sweet basil
Salt and pepper

Peel and seed pumpkin and cut into cubes. Put everything into a large kettle and add enough water to cover plus 2" additional. Cook over medium heat until beans and pumpkin are tender. Good served with warm tortillas and salsa.

Pumpkin Basque Style

1 small pumpkin, top cut out (save for a lid), seeded and membranes removed
1 lb. rice, uncooked
2 lbs. medium shrimp, sautéed in butter
1 medium grated onion
1 large green pepper, seeded and chopped
3 cloves of garlic, peeled and chopped
2 tbsps. butter
salt and pepper

Place rice in pumpkin, put the rest of the ingredients on top of the rice, put the rest of the ingredients on top of the rice and sprinkle with salt and pepper. Cover rice mixture with enough water to just cover plus about 1" more on top. Put lid on and put pumpkin in baking pan. Bake at 325° for 1-

1/2 hr - 2 hr or until rice mix is fully cooked and pumpkin is tender.

Note: This dish is traditionally served on November 1st in the Spanish and French Basque countries. This would be very good served with hot sourdough bread.

Sauces

The sauce recipe following goes back to our early founders' days. The words are as it was written early on. Accordingly, it is called:

Pumpkin "Sause"

"The Housewives' manner is to slice them when ripe and cute them into dice, and so fill a pot with them in two or three gallons and stew them upon a gentle fire the whole day. And as they sink they fill again with fresh Pompions not putting any liquor to them and when it is stirred enough it will look like baked apples, this dish putting butter to it and a little vinegar with some spice as ginger which makes it tart like an apple, and so serve it up to be eaten with fish or flesh."[8]

Pumpkinseed Mole

1 c. hulled pumpkinseeds
1 small onion, diced
2 tbsps. peanut butter
1 c. chicken broth
1-1/2 c. tomato sauce
2 cloves garlic, chopped
2 tbsp. masa harina
t tap. nutmeg
1 tsp. salt

Put all ingredients except chicken broth through blender until smooth. Add pureed mixture to the chicken broth in a saucepan; heat and simmer for 10 minutes, stirring occasionally to blend. Serve hot. Makes about 2-1/2 c. sauce. Good with chicken or seafood cooked in the sauce.

Pumpkin Sauce for Chicken

3/4 c. shelled pumpkin seeds
2 wide chilies
2 narrow chilies
1/2 c. dry slivered almonds
1 c. popped corn
3 c. chicken broth
1 clove garlic, minced
1/2 c. cilantro, chopped fine
1/2 c. bacon grease
salt and pepper

Wash chilies and remove seeds, saving them. Take care not to rub your eyes and not to handle chilies more than necessary. It would be a good idea to even wear gloves to avoid an accident.

Soak chilies in warm water for 25 minutes. Meanwhile, toast pumpkinseeds, almonds and chili seeds in a dry skillet. Grind in a blender with popped corn and garlic to make a fine paste. Add in chicken broth a little at a time, stirring constantly. Continue to cook sauce over medium heat until it becomes thick. Then remove from heat and put in a bowl. Heat bacon grease in skillet thoroughly, then add sauce mixture back in. Add cilantro, salt and pepper and cooked turkey or chicken and simmer for about 15 min.

Pumpkin Raisin Seed Sauce

1/2 lb. pumpkin seeds, shelled
1/2 c. seedless raisins
1/2 lb. dried California chilies
3 cloves garlic
1-1/2 c. chicken stock
1 c. water
1/2 c. sour cream
1 tsp. ea. nutmeg and cinnamon

Soak pumpkin seeds in water overnight. Drain and put into blender with one cup of the chicken stock, puree until smooth. Remove from blender and set aside. Remove stems and seeds from chilies, taking precautions not to rub your eyes or face while working with them. Place in one cup of water in a pot and bring to a boil. Remove from heat; add the pureed pumpkinseeds, garlic and spices. Stir until smooth. Sauce consistency should be like heavy cream. Add sour cream and raisins. Makes about 3 cups. This sauce goes well with pork or chicken.

Pumpkin Salsa

1/4 c. toasted pumpkinseeds
4 sm. green or red chilies
1/2 sm. onion, diced
1 c. stewed tomatoes
2 c. chicken stock
2 tbsp. olive oil
1/4 c. chopped cilantro
1/2 c. fresh chopped parsley
salt and pepper

Put pumpkin seeds, chilies, stewed tomatoes, onions, parsley and cilantro through blender until almost liquid in consistency. Add the stock. Heat oil in a deep pan and add sauce mixture and seasonings. Bring to a boil, reduce heat and simmer five minutes more, stirring constantly. Serve with chick, pork, fish, beans, chips, or cooked rice.

Peanut-Pumpkin Sauce

1 c. mashed, cooked pumpkin
2 tbsps. peanut butter
1/2 c. water
salt

Blend ingredients together and serve with vegetable dishes or on bread. Makes 1-1/2 cups.

Pumpkin Sauce with Dates

1 c. mashed pumpkin
1/2 c. pitted dates
1 c. apple cider
1/4 c. honey
1 tbsp. lemon juice
2 tbsp. butter
1 tsp. allspice

In a saucepan, gently mix all ingredients and heat thoroughly. Good over ice cream or vanilla pudding.

Pumpkin Pear Sauce

10 medium pears, seeded and cubed
1/2 small pumpkin, peeled, seeded and cubed
1-1/2 c. sugar
2 tbsps. grated orange rind
1 tsp. cinnamon
1 tsp. nutmeg

Put fruit into a heavy saucepan with the sugar, orange rind and spices. Cover and simmer about an hour, stirring occasionally until fruits are tender. Put through blender until mixture has the consistency of applesauce and then chill.

Jams, Pickles, Drinks & Other Good Things

Pumpkin Jam

4 lbs. pumpkins, peeled, seeded and diced
2 lbs. sugar
Juice of 3 lemons and grated peel
1 tbsps. ginger & allspice
1/4 c. sweet gin (optional)

Place pumpkin in large bowl, alternating with layers of sugar. Cover with cheesecloth and let stand two days in a cool place. Place in large saucepan with ginger, allspice, lemon peel and juice. Simmer over medium heat, stirring often, until pumpkin is tender and transparent. Remove from heat, cool slightly and add gin. Stir thoroughly. Pour into sterilized jars. Seal and Makes 6 – 8 quarts.

Old-Fashioned Pumpkin Marmalade

5 lbs. pumpkin, seeded and cut into strips
3 lemons with zest
2 oranges with zest
4 lbs. sugar
1 tsp. each cinnamon, nutmeg

Cover pumpkin with sugar and let stand overnight. Put lemons and orange through juicer and add juice and spices to pumpkin. Stir over low heat until boiling, then simmer until thick and clear, stirring frequently to prevent scorching. Process takes 1-1/2 - 2 hours. Seal in hot sterilized jars.

Candied Pumpkin

1 small pumpkin - (not miniature)
1 c. brown sugar
1 c. unsweetened pineapple juice
4 pieces candied ginger, sliced thin

Cut the pumpkin in half, peeling it and removing seeds and membranes. Cut into medium thick slices. Boil sugar and pineapple juice until it forms a syrup. Add pumpkin and ginger, cooking until tender. Turn off heat; let pumpkin and ginger marinate overnight in syrup. Drain the syrup and cook until it forms a thread when drizzled from spoon. Add pumpkin once more, simmering it until it is thick and clear. Drain pumpkin slices on a plate, saving the syrup. Place pumpkin on a cheesecloth covered rack in a warm place. Dry until it is tender and no longer sticky - about 24 hours. Candied pumpkin can be used in the fruitcake recipe in the dessert section, or you could use it in fruited breads and cookies. You can use the syrup over ice cream or on toast.

Pumpkin Conserve

1 sm. pumpkin, peeled, seeded and cubed
1 lb. ea. dried apricots and seedless raisins
1 lb. sugar
2 tbsps. lemon juice
2 tbsps. chopped crystallized ginger

Alternate pumpkin cubes with sugar and let stand overnight. Wash and cut apricots into pieces, adding to the pumpkins. Add raisins, lemon juice and ginger, simmering until the pumpkin is transparent and tender. Put into sterilized jars and seal.

Pickled Pumpkin

1 sm. pumpkin, peeled and cubed
1 pint cider vinegar
5 lbs. sugar
1 tsp. cinnamon stick, broken
2 pieces crystallized ginger
1 tsp. whole cloves

Bring vinegar and sugar to a boil and simmer until the sugar is dissolved. Add cloves, cinnamon and ginger to the syrup and boil 4 minutes. Add the pumpkin and bring the mixture back to a boil. Turn down heat and continue to simmer until pumpkin is tender and clear. Put the pumpkin into sterilized jars, pouring in syrup to completely cover and seal.

Pumpkin Flour

Pumpkin flour, made by grinding up dried pumpkin slices, can be used along with regular wheat flour to add moisture, color and extra food value to baked goods.

Clean and cut a small or medium pumpkin (depending on how much pumpkin flour you want to end up with) into 1" strips, then remove the peel. Boil in a large saucepan for 10 minutes or until slightly soft. Dry pumpkin in whatever manner you prefer -- the sun, a dehydrator, or even the oven on low heat. When pumpkin is thoroughly dry, pasteurize slices by placing in a 175° oven for 45 minutes. Grind into coarse meal in a blender. Store the flour in airtight containers in a cool, dry place (preferably in the refrigerator or freezer).

Pumpkin Brew

1 large pumpkin
Juice from 2 lemons
2 large boxes raisins
1 c. brown sugar
2 cakes yeast (or 2 packages dried)

Cut the top of the pumpkin off, removing seeds and membranes. Fill cavity with sugar, lemon juice, raising and yeast. Set the pumpkin in a glass pan, allowing the mixture to work until the flesh of the pumpkin dissolves, then strain through until the flesh of the pumpkin dissolves, then strain through several layers of cheesecloth. Allow yeast to settle, then strain once more. Bottle the liquid, making sure it has stopped fermenting before corking (It will no longer bubble). Makes about 2-1/2 quarts. Refrigerate and serve when cool.

This brew is similar to the substitute "beer" made by early colonists. They used pumpkin, persimmons and maple syrup, but as yeast was not readily available, it probably was not used.

Pumpkin Shake

My friend used to make healthy fruit shakes this way, and I love the idea, so I adapted it for pumpkin.

1 lg. can pumpkin
1 tsp. cinnamon
1/2 tsp. ea. nutmeg, allspice
1/4 c. brown sugar

Mix all ingredients and divide into 4 parts. Put into freezer containers and freeze.

When you are ready for a milkshake, get out one frozen container and put it into the blender (keep frozen). Add 1 egg, and 1-1/2 c. milk and add 1 tsp. nutritional yeast (optional, but very good and very healthy. Blend until pumpkin is well blended and there are no chunks. Pour into large glass and serve.

Pumpkin Punch

This is a truly refreshing punch, perfect for a party.

1 lg. can pumpkin
1-1/2 c. light cream
2 eggs
2 lg. bottles ginger ale, chilled
1/4 c. brown sugar
1-1/2 tsp. pumpkin pie spice

Combine pumpkin, light cream, eggs, sugar and spices and blend until smooth. Chill. When you are ready to serve, pour into punch bowl and add ginger ale, pouring slowly onto the inside of the bowl to save the bubbles. You can float small scoops of vanilla ice cream on top just before serving, but if the punch is going to sit before people drink it, you might want to have the ice cream available for people to scoop into their own cups.

Pumpkin Soap

1 - 8 oz. can pumpkin
6 oz. pumpkin pie fragrance oil (available from a soap making supply store)
22 oz coconut oil
22.4 oz. olive oil
16 oz. sunflower oil

(Note: if you are unable to find any of the above oil types, you CAN substitute other oils that are similar. Again, health food stores or soap making supply stores should have most of these).

4 oz. Shea butter (This should be available from a soap making supply store or health food supply - not edible, but used in cosmetics)
10 oz. lye
16 oz. Water
4 oz. of pumpkin pie fragrance oil
2 tsps. allspice

Melt your oils to 100°. You can check this with a candy thermometer. In a separate pot, add 3 tsps. sugar and 1-1/2 tsp. salt to the water, before adding the lye. Heat and blend until it is liquid soap. Separate out some of the soap and add the pumpkin and fragrance oil. Add the spice. Blend the two mixes - the pumpkin and the lye mixture very lightly so that you get a sort of marble effect. Pour into the mold and allow it to cool and dry adequately. If you live where there is a lot of moisture in the air, it might take a little longer to dry properly. When cool you can get it out and slice it if you need to and wrap it in some pretty paper and seal it so you can keep it dry and also it will make nice gifts.

Glycerin Pumpkin Soap

4 oz. glycerin soap (clear & unscented). You can use a bar of soap, which you can purchase inexpensively or you can also purchase liquid glycerin, which will not need to be melted as with the bar of soup.
1/4 tsp. pumpkin fragrance oil
6 drops of nutmeg essential oil (An essential oil is a natural chemical extracted from the leaves, flowers, stems, roots or bark of plants. It is not a true oil; it is the aromatic and volatile essences derived from these plant parts.)
1/2 tsp. ground cloves

To get the color, mix yellow and red food coloring to get an orange - a little goes a long way. In a small saucepan over low heat (or in a glass measuring cup in the microwave) melt glycerin soap (unless you are using the liquid). Add the nutmeg essential oil, pumpkin fragrance oil, ground cloves and food coloring, stirring well. Pour into mold or molds and allow the mixture to set. Remove from mold, then wrap pumpkin pie soap in cellophane or plastic wrap to keep additional moisture out. You can also wrap it in pretty paper for gift giving.

Sweet Things

Puddings

Pumpkin Bread Pudding

3/4 cup canned pureed pumpkin
1 cup heavy cream (or low fat half and half)
1/2 c. golden raisins
1/2 cup whole milk
1/2 cup sugar (or sugar substitute in appropriate amount)
2 large eggs plus 1 yolk (you can use the egg substitute for this
Salt
1/2 tsp. ea. ground cinnamon, ginger, allspice, and cloves
5 c. cubed (1-inch cubes) crusty bread
3/4 stick butter, melted

Preheat oven to 350°F. Mix pumpkin, raisins, cream, milk, sugar, eggs, yolk, salt, and spices in a bowl.

Toss bread cubes with butter in another bowl, then add pumpkin mixture and toss to coat. Transfer to an ungreased 8-inch square baking dish on the middle rack and bake until set, 25 to 30 minutes. You could add 1/2 c. chopped walnuts or pecans to the mix as well for a variety.

Pumpkin Coconut Pudding

1 lg. can pumpkin
2 c. light cream
2 eggs, separated
1/2 c. brown sugar
2/4 c. flour
1/2 c. coconut
1/2 c. walnuts or pecans, chopped
1 tsp. vanilla
1 tsp. cinnamon
1/2 tsp. ea. nutmeg, ginger, allspice

Combine dry ingredients. Add pumpkin and mix well. Beat in egg yolks and slowly add milk. Stir in coconut and nuts. In a small bowl, beat egg whites until peaks form. Fold into pumpkin mixture. Put into oiled casserole dish and bake in 350° preheated oven for 50 - 60 minutes, or until knife inserted comes out clean. Serve warm or cold and of course, whipped cream is always good.

Pumpkin Flan

1 c. canned pumpkin
2 c. light cream
3 lg. eggs, separated
1 c. brown sugar, divided in half
1 tsp. vanilla extract
1 tsp. pumpkin pie spice

Sprinkle 1/2 cup sugar into a 9-inch metal round cake pan. Cook over medium-high heat, shaking pan occasionally using oven mitts, until sugar melts and turns a light golden brown; set aside and allow it to cool. Heat milk and remaining sugar in a heavy saucepan, stirring constantly, until hot and frothy. Set aside.

Beat egg whites until they have a good body. Add eggs and other half of sugar, vanilla and spice and beat until well blended; gradually adding hot milk mixture, and continuing to beat until mixture is smooth.. Pour this mixture over caramelized sugar in the cake pan. Place cake pan in a roasting pan with 1 inch of water.

Bake at 350° for 1 hour or until a knife inserted in center of flan comes out clean. Remove pan from water; and cool on a wire rack. Cover and chill. Loosen edges of flan with a spatula, and invert onto a serving plate.

Pumpkin Rice Pudding

1 lg. can pumpkin
2 eggs
1-2/3 c. light cream
2/3 c. instant rice, uncooked
1/2 c. brown sugar, packed
1/2 c. raisins
1 tsp. pumpkin pie spice
1 tsp. grated orange rind
salt

Combine sugar, spices, salt and pumpkin and set aside. In a separate bowl, beat the eggs with the light cream. Add to pumpkin mixture, then add the remaining ingredients. Spoon pudding mixture into oiled casserole dish. Place casserole dish inside a pan of water (example, you can use a cake pan). Bake in a preheated 350o oven for 50 - 60 minutes, stirring occasionally. Test by inserting a knife in center, and it should come out clean. You can serve warm or cold, and add dollops of whipped cream on top.

Indian Pumpkin Pudding

Indian pudding was one of my favorite dishes that my Mom made. When I started creating recipes for the book, I thought about making one with pumpkin in it. Oh, what a delight!!!

1 c. canned pumpkin
1/4 c. cornmeal
3 c. light cream
1 c. water
1 lg. egg, lightly beaten
1/2 cup molasses
1/3 cup dark brown sugar, firmly packed
1 tbsp. butter
1 tsp. ground ginger
1/2 tsp. ea. allspice and cloves
1/2 tsp. salt

Preheat oven to 325°. Mix cornmeal with water in a small bowl. Transfer to a heavy saucepan and stir in 2 cups of the milk and salt. Bring to a boil, stirring constantly, then reduce the heat to medium and continue to stir 10 minutes or until thick and smooth. Remove from heat and stir in remaining ingredients except remaining cup of milk. Pour into oiled casserole dish and bake for 30 minutes.

Remove and stir in the last cup of milk. Return to oven and bake 1-1/2 hours longer, until thick and bubbly. Serve warm. My mom served this with dollops of whipped cream.

Pumpkin Coffee Mousse

1 lg. cans pumpkin
6 c. heavy whipping cream
1-1/2 c. brown sugar (reserve 1/4 c. for later use)
8 tsps. instant coffee
1 tsp. cinnamon
1/2 tsp. nutmeg and allspice

Mix pumpkin with 1-1/4 c. of the brown sugar and cook over medium heat, stirring constantly until sugar is completely dissolved. Add coffee and spices and mix well. Set aside to cool thoroughly. Meanwhile, beat whipping cream with ¼ cup sugar until peaks hold shape. Fold the whipped cream into the pumpkin mixture. Spoon the mousses into serving dishes and chill for at least 2 hours before serving. You can put a dollop of whipped cream on each serving topped with half a pecan or walnut if desired.

Pumpkin Custard

1 lg. can pumpkin
1-1/2 c. light cream
2 eggs
1/2 c. brown sugar
1 tsp. cinnamon
1/2 tsp. ea. ginger, nutmeg

Combine milk, eggs, sugar and spices., mixing well. Add pumpkin and stir until smooth and well blended. Pour into individual 6 oz. custard cups and bake at 350° for 50 minutes, or until knife inserted in center comes out clean. This should give you 6 servings.

Pumpkin Yogurt Custard

3 c. canned pumpkin
1/2 c. vanilla yogurt
2 eggs
1/4 c. brown sugar
2 tbsps. lemon juice
1 tsp. cinnamon
1/2 tsp. ea. nutmeg, ginger, allspice

Combine all ingredients, stirring until consistently blended. Pour custard mix into 6 individual oiled baking dishes. Bake at 350° for 40 min. or until knife inserted in center comes out clean.

Pumpkin Chocolate Pudding

1 lg. can pumpkin
1-6 oz. instant chocolate pudding
1/4 c. powdered cocoa
1-1/2 c. light cream
1 tsp. cinnamon
1/2 tsp. ea. nutmeg, cloves and ginger
2 c. heavy whipping cream, whipped until it has peaks

Add light cream to pudding mix and add cocoa. Beat according to package directions, then put bowl in refrigerator for 10 minutes. Add pumpkin and spices and mix well. Put into dessert bowls and top with the whipped cream before serving. You can get four servings out of this.

Plumpkin' Pudding

I absolutely love plum pudding, which my mom used to serve every Thanksgiving and Christmas. Hers was the canned plum pudding, but I always wanted to learn how to make it. This opportunity to do it with pumpkin was definitely the right choice.

1 lg. can pumpkin
2 eggs, well beaten
1/4 cup milk
1/4 cup apple juice
1 c. all-purpose flour
1/4 pound ground suet (you can substitute butter if you cannot get suet)
1 teaspoon baking soda
1 cup brown sugar, packed
1 tsp. cinnamon
1/2 tsp. ea. nutmeg, cloves, ginger
1 tsp. salt
 1 cup raisins
1 1/2 cup dried cranberries
2 cups mixed cut-up dried fruits (plums, apricots, apples, pineapple, or ones you like best)
1/2 cup finely chopped pecans, walnuts, or almonds
1/4 cup all-purpose flour
1 cup soft day-old bread crumbs

Sift together all dry ingredients except the 1/4 c. flour and bread crumbs. Set aside. Separately mix pumpkin, suet or butter, sugar, milk and cider; and eggs. Mix the raisins, cranberries, mixed dried fruit and nuts with the 1/4 cup flour, then add to the pumpkin and suet mixture. Add in the crumbs and remaining dried ingredients, mix well.

Turn into oiled and floured 2-quart pudding mold or 2 1-pound coffee cans. Cover with 2 thicknesses of wax paper, allowing space for pudding to rise. Tie tightly.

Place on rack in a large pan or Dutch oven with a tight fitting lid. Place mold or coffee cans inside. Pour in enough boiling water to come half way up the outside of the mold or coffee cans. Cover and bring water to boil, then turn heat down and simmer and steam 2 1/2 hours. I always check the water to make sure there is still plenty there and replenish if the water has gotten low.

When Plumkin' Pudding is done, remove from heat and turn out onto a serving dish or large bowl. You could serve with dollops of whipped cream or hard sauce (recipe below).

Hard Sauce for Pudding

1/4 lb. butter
8 oz, powdered sugar
6 oz. rum

Melt butter in saucepan and begin beating in powdered sugar until it is smooth, then stir in rum.

Cookies

Pumpkin Peanut Butter Cookies

1 sm. can pumpkin puree
1-1/2 c. unbleached flour
1 c. brown sugar
1/2 c. peanut butter
1/2 c. butter
2 eggs + egg yolk from one egg (save this for brushing tops of cookies)
1 tsp. cinnamon
1/2 tsp. ea. ground nutmeg, ginger, mace
1-1/2 tsp. baking powder
Unshelled unsalted peanuts if desired for garnishing

Preheat oven to 350°. Combine dry ingredients, mixing thoroughly. Blend in eggs, butter, pumpkin and peanut butter, adding a tiny bit of water if necessary to form a smooth dough. Knead lightly until dough is elastic in texture. Roll out on a floured board until 1/3" thick approx. and cut into small rounds (or squares or rectangles if you wish so you won't have the leftover dough between the rounds to deal with). How many cookies you get depends on whether you are cutting large pieces or small. Personally, large cookies taste best to me! Place rounds on oiled cookie sheet and brush tops of cookies with egg yolk. You can put one unsalted peanut in the top of each cookie if desired. Bake for 10 - 12 minutes or until golden brown.

Chunkin' Pumpkin Cookies

1 sm. can pumpkin
1-1/2 c. flour
1 c. oats
2 eggs
1 c. brown sugar
1 c. raisins
3/4 c. chocolate chips
1/2 c. coconut
1/2 c. chopped nuts
2 tsps. baking powder
1/2 tsp. salt
1-1/2 tsp. pumpkin pie spice
1 tsp. vanilla
1 tsp. lemon extract

Preheat oven to 375°. Cream butter and sugar and beat in eggs and pumpkin. Stir in vanilla and lemon extract. Mix raisins, chocolate chips, coconut and chopped nuts with remaining dry ingredients and add to pumpkin mixture, stirring until dough is totally mixed. Drop by spoonfuls onto oiled or Teflon baking sheet (use either a tsp. or a tbsp. depending on whether you like your cookies big or small). Bake 15 min. or until cookies are golden brown. Cookie making isn't an exact science, and how quickly your cookies are ready depends on your particular oven, the elevation, and probably how many dust balls are on the floor. Just keep your eyes on them as they are baking; check them after say 8 minutes, and then again every few minutes.

Golden Pumpkin Health Cookies

1 sm. can pumpkin
2 c. unbleached flour
2 tbs. Yellow cornmeal
1/4 c. flax flour or you can use wheat germ if you are unable to obtain flax flour
1 c. powdered milk
2 eggs, beaten
1/3 c. vegetable oil
1/2 c. molasses
1/3 c. apple or orange juice
1 tsp. cinnamon
1/2 tsp. ea. nutmeg, ginger, ground cloves

Preheat oven to 350°. Blend molasses and oil. Add remainder of ingredients. Batter should be stiff. If too thick, add unsweetened fruit juice; if too think, add more flour. Drop by teaspoonfuls onto oiled or Teflon baking sheet. Bake for 12 - 15 min. or until golden brown. For a variation, add 1/2 c. pitted chopped prunes, or 1/2 c. raisins with 2 tbsps. grated orange or lemon rind. You may also substitute oatmeal for half the flour.

Pumpkin Pie Squares

1 sm. can pumpkin
1 c. unbleached flour
1 c. rolled oats
1/2 c. butter
2 eggs
1 can evaporated milk
1 c. brown sugar
1 tsp. cinnamon

1/2 tsp. ea. ginger, powered cloves
Save separately for top:
1/2 c. brown sugar
1/2 c. chopped pecans
2 tbsps. butter

Combine dry ingredients and butter in medium bowl, mixing until crumbly. Press into 13" x 9" x 2" pan. Bake in 350° oven for 15 minutes. Combine pumpkin, milk and eggs and pour onto crust. Combine pecans, 1/2 c. brown sugar and 2 tbsps. butter and sprinkle over pumpkin filling. Bake for 15 - 20 min. more, or until filling is set.

Pumpkin Sunflower Seed Bars

1 sm. can pumpkin
4 c. unbleached flour
1 egg
1/2 c. dry milk
1 c. brown sugar
1/2 c. sunflower seeds
1 tsp. vanilla
2 tsps. baking powder
1 tsp. baking soda
1 tsp. cinnamon
1/2 tsp. ea. powdered nutmeg, cloves, allspice, ginger

Preheat oven to 400°. Mix all dry ingredients and then pour in pumpkin and egg and vanilla. Pour into a 13 x 9 x 2" oiled baking pan and bake for 12 - 15 minutes, or until golden brown. Cut into bars.

For a variation, add 1/2 c. cut-up dates or raisins.

Pumpkin Empanadas

2 c. all purpose flour
2/3 c. butter
4 tbsps. cold water
salt
filling mixture
1/2 c. sugar and 1 tsp. cinnamon, mixed

Blend dry ingredients in a bowl. Cut butter into flour with fork or pastry blender. Sprinkle water evenly over the top of mixture and mix evenly with a fork. Turn out on waxed paper. Chill for 1/2 - 1 hour. Roll out chilled dough 1/4" thick and cut into 4 - 5" circles. Spoon filling on one side of each circle. Moisten edges, fold in half and press edges together with a fork. Brush with butter. Bake in a 400° oven for 20 minutes, or until browned. You can roll empanadas in sugar mixed with cinnamon. Makes 12 – 15.

Filling

1 sm. can. Pumpkin
1/2 c. brown sugar, packed
1/2 c. raisins
2 tbsps. cinnamon

Blend mixture in a medium saucepan and heat well, stirring constantly to prevent burning. Cool before using.

Pumpkin Poppy-Seed Cookies

1 sm. can pumpkin
2-1/2 c. all-purpose flour
3/4 c. butter
1 egg

1-1/2 c. brown sugar
1/4 c. light molasses
1 c. finely chopped pecans
1/3 c. poppy seeds.
1 tsp. vanilla
1 tsp. baking powder
1 tsp. baking soda
salt

Cream sugar and butter and add egg, pumpkin, molasses and vanilla into mixture. Add dry ingredients, blending until smooth. Stir in pecans and poppy seeds. Drop by rounded teaspoonfuls onto cookie sheet. Bake at 350° for 10-12 minutes until golden brown. Let cool and frost if desired.

Pumpkin Chocolate Chip Cookies

1 sm. can pumpkin
1 sm. package chocolate chips
1 c. chopped nuts
4 c. unbleached flour
2 beaten eggs
1/4 c. milk
1 c. vegetable oil
1 c. brown sugar
1 tsp. baking soda
1 tsp. baking powder
1/2 tsp. salt
1 tsp. cinnamon
1 tsp. nutmeg
1 tsp. ground ginger
1 tsp. allspice
2 tsp. vanilla

Mix dry ingredients and then add in eggs, milk, vegetable oil and vanilla and stir until mixture is totally blended. Drop by teaspoonfuls (or tbsps. to give you bigger cookies). Bake at 375° for 12 - 15 minutes or until golden brown. You can vary this by using butterscotch chips instead of the chocolate chips.

Pumpkin Bars

Pastry for Bars

1 c. all-purpose flour
1/2 c. butter
4 lg. eggs
1 c. water
salt

In a medium saucepan, bring water and butter to a boil and continue heating until butter is melted. Remove from heat and add flour and salt. Stir mixture over low heat for 1 minute. Cool for a few minutes, then add 4 eggs one at a time, beating well after each addition. Divide pastry into two halves and spread each half onto an oiled cookie sheet, each half being 6" square when ready. Bake at 400° for 45 min. or until golden brown. Turn oven off and return pastry to oven, leaving door open. Leave in the oven an additional 15 min. Meanwhile, make the filling.

Filling for Bars

1 sm. can pumpkin
1 c. whipped cream
1/2 c. brown sugar, packed
2 tbsps. orange juice and grated orange rind

2 tbsps. cinnamon
1/2 tsp. ea. ground ginger and nutmeg
Small amount of candied ginger for garnish

Mix filling ingredients, folding in the well beaten whipped cream last. Divide the filling evenly between the two pastry holders and place the lids on top. Serve with extra amounts of whipped cream and bits of candied ginger.

Piecrusts

I generally use prepared piecrusts. They work fine for me and come two to a package, but you might want to have a recipe for piecrusts that are homemade. Some of the recipes here have special crusts like graham cracker crusts, and those are included with the general recipes. Here are a few basic crust recipes for your pies.

Basic Piecrust

1 1/3 cup all-purpose flour
1/2 cup shortening
1/2 tsp. coarse salt
3 tsps. ice water

Mix flour and salt in mixing bowl. Cut shortening into the flour with a pastry cutter, until mixture resembles the texture of tiny split peas. You need to use the pastry cutter and not your hands or you will have a mess with the shortening getting too warm. Maybe all this work is why I always use the prepared piecrusts.

When mixture is the right consistency, add ice water and mix with a fork. Even if it seems like it needs more water, resist the temptation. Roll the dough into a ball and flatten into a 4-inch-wide disk. Wrap in plastic, and refrigerate for 1/2 hour minimum.

Remove dough disk from refrigerator. If stiff and very cold, let stand until dough is cool but you can work with it.

Flour a countertop area or chopping board and roll the rolling pin in the flour. Roll the dough disk on a lightly floured surface from the center out in each direction, forming a 12-inch circle. To transfer dough, carefully roll it around the rolling pin, lift and unroll dough, centering it in an ungreased 9-inch pie plate.

Makes 1 9-inch pie crust. Double the recipe for a two-crust pie. Although piecrusts ARE time-consuming to make, they are very therapeutic, and you can cover them and freeze them for future pies using the aluminum pie crust pans you can purchase cheaply at grocery stores.

Oatmeal Piecrust

1 c. quick-cooking oats
1-c. all-purpose flour
1/2 c. powdered sugar
1/2 tsp. pumpkin pie spice
1/4 teaspoon salt
1/4 cup butter, melted
2 tablespoons vegetable shortening, melted

Preheat oven to 350°F. Combine oats, flour, powdered sugar, pumpkin pie spice and salt. Stir in butter and shortening.

Oil a 9-inch pie pan; press oatmeal mixture into bottom and up sides.

Bake for 20 minutes or until golden brown. Cool for a minimum of 10 minutes, then fill with pie filling, following directions to cook pie with filling if appropriate.

Nut Piecrust

2 1/2 c. finely ground walnuts or pecans
1/2 tsp. ea. cinnamon, nutmeg
1/3 c. brown sugar
1/4 c. butter, melted

Stir together nuts, cinnamon and sugar, mix in melted butter. Press mixture onto the bottom and up the sides of a 9- Chill the for about 30 to 45 minutes.

Bake in a preheated 350° oven for 12 minutes, or until lightly browned. Watch carefully; nut crusts burn easily. Cool completely before filling. The filling should be precooked so that it doesn't have to be baked for any more time.

Pies

Dutch Pumpkin Pie
(from a Mennonite friend many years ago)

Line a medium size pie tin with pastry, covered thickly with 2 c. thinly sliced, uncooked pumpkin cut in 1" lengths.

Over the top of the pumpkin sprinkle 1 tbsp. flour, 1 tbsp. molasses, 1 tsp. vinegar and 4 tbsps. light brown sugar.

Dust over the top a small quantity of ground cinnamon, cloves and ground nutmeg (use the amount that appeals to you). Add top crust and the bake the pie in a moderately hot oven. When baked, the pumpkin filling in the pie resembles and tastes like sliced citron.

Caramelized Pumpkin Pie

1 lg. plus 1 sm. cans pumpkin
4 large eggs, slightly beaten
3 c. light cream, scalded
1 c. whipped cream flavored with vanilla (1 tsp. min. or more depending on how strong you like the taste of vanilla)
1 tbsp. butter
1-1/2 c. brown sugar, packed
1/2 c. pecan halves
2 tbsps. molasses
2 tsps. cinnamon
1 tsp. ground ginger
1/2 tsp. nutmeg
1 unbaked 9" pie shell

In a medium saucepan, caramelize the sugar over medium-high heat until it is a deep golden brown. Add pecans and stir to coat them. Add the butter and remove the pan from the heat. Stir the nuts until the butter is totally blended in. Spread the caramelized mixture evenly over the bottom of the piecrust. Set aside.

Preheat the oven to 425°. In a large bowl whisk together the pumpkin, cream, and eggs until smooth. Add the remaining ingredients (except the whipped cream, which is reserved for serving on top of slices,) and stir well until smooth. Pour over the caramelized mixture.

Bake for 15 minutes at 425°. Lower the heat to 350° and continue to bake for 30–40 minutes until the custard is set, or until a knife inserted in the center comes out clean. Remove from the oven and cool before cutting.

All-American Pumpkin Pie

Everyone has his or her favorite pumpkin pie recipe, and this is a somewhat basic one, but it gives you some ideas for putting some pizzazz into a pretty decent pumpkin pie if you choose.

1 lg. can pumpkin
3 c. light cream
1 c. whipping cream
2 eggs
1 c. brown sugar
2 tbsps. flour
1 tsp. cinnamon

1 tsp. allspice
1/2 tsp. powdered ginger, nutmeg and cloves
1 9" pie shell, unbaked

Put the pumpkin in a large bowl and sprinkle it with the 2 tbsps. flour, stirring in the sugar as well. Add the light cream and bring to a boil. Remove from heat and add seasonings and heavy cream. Add the beaten eggs and stir together until the mixture is well blended.

Extra for All-American Pumpkin Pie

2 tbsps. sugar
1 tbsp. flour

Mix the extra flour and sugar and sprinkle it over the bottom of the pie shell. Fill the pie shells with the pumpkin mixture and cover edges of crust with aluminum foil to keep them from browning too fast. Bake 15 min. at 450°,

then reduce heat to 325° and bake about half an hour or until knife inserted in the center comes out clean.

For a variation, substitute 1/2 c. sour cream for an equal amount of the light cream. Just before serving, spread the pie with 6 - 8 tbsps. plum jam or orange marmalade, then serve with dollops of whipped cream.

Pumpkin Pie with Butterscotch Sauce

1 sm. can pumpkin
1 c. light cream, scalded
2 eggs, beaten slightly

1/3 c. sugar
1 tbsp. butter
2 tsps. pumpkin pie spice
salt
1 9" pie crust

Add butter to scalded milk. Mix eggs with sugar and add to pumpkin mixture. Add salt and seasonings to pumpkin. Pour into unbaked piecrust and bake in preheated 450° oven for about 10 - 12 minutes to set crust. Then lower heat to about 400° for about 5 minutes. As crust begins to turn light brown on edges, lower heat to 300° (if filling begins to bubble, turn heat down to 275°). Bake until a knife blade inserted in the center comes out clean. Serve with butterscotch sauce below.

Butterscotch Sauce

1-1/4 c. brown sugar
1/3 c. dark corn syrup
1 pint heavy cream, whipped
3/4 c. light cream
4 tbsps. butter
1 tsp. vanilla
1 tsp. rum flavoring

Mix brown sugar, syrup and butter in pan and bring to a boil, stirring constantly until syrup forms a soft ball in cold water. Remove from heat and immediately pour in 3/4 c. think cream. Beat cream into the syrup until thoroughly mixed. Pour into jars, leaving a 2" space at the top for mixing the sauce before it is served. Cover and refrigerate. This sauce keeps indefinitely under refrigeration.

Pumpkin-Persimmon Pie

1 sm. can pumpkin
2/3 c. persimmon pulp
3 eggs, slightly beaten
1 - 14 oz. can sweetened condensed milk
1/2 c. brown sugar, packed
1 tsp. cinnamon
1/2 tsp. ea. nutmeg, cloves, ground ginger
salt
1 unbaked 9" pie shell

Mix all ingredients until well blended and pour into the pie shell. Bake at 350° for 45 minutes or until center is firm when knife is inserted in center. Serve with shipped cream and sprinkles of chopped nuts.

Pumpkin Pye Recipe from *The Compleat Cook*, by W.M. London, 1655[1]

"To make a Pumpion Pye, take about half a pound of Pumpion and slice it, adding a handful of Tyme, a little Rosemary, Parsley and Sweet Marjorum slipped off the stalks, and chop them small then take Cynamon, Nutmeg, Pepper, and six Cloves, and beat them. Take ten Egges and beat them, then mix them, and beat them altogether, and put in as much Sugar as you think fit. Then fry them like a Froize, after it is fryed, let it stand till it be cold. Then fill your Pye, take slices Apples thinner round wayes, and lay a row of the Froize, add a layer of Apples with Currants between the layer while your Pye is fitted, and put in a good deal of sweet Butter before you close it. When the Pye is baked, take 6 yelks of Eggs, some white wine or Vergas and make a caudle of this, but not thick, butt up the lid and put it in. Stir them well together whilst the Eggs and Pumpions be not perceived and so serve it up."

From the research I have done, a froize was something like an omelet of eggs, often combined with eggs and then fried until fairly solid. Notice how the ingredients were included right in the text and often not very specific as to how much of anything should be used or temperatures as there was no real temperature control.

You were pretty much trusting fate when you cooked then. And with no refrigeration either, things had to be eaten up right after they were cooked. Caudle in this sense means a warm drink consisting of wine or ale mixed with sugar, eggs, bread, and various spices, sometimes given to ill persons. It is interesting that they put pepper and also herbs into the pie with the other ingredients, likely to try to preserve them since they had no way to preserve what was cooked unless it was eaten right away.

Pumpkin-Apple Pie

Pumpkin Layer

1 sm. can pumpkins
2 eggs, slightly beaten
1 c. light cream, scalded
2 eggs, slightly beaten
1/2 c. brown sugar, packed
2 tbsps. butter or margarine, melted
1 tsp. cinnamon
1 tsp. ginger
1/2 tsp. ground cloves

Apple Layer

2 c. peeled, cored, and thinly sliced green apples
1/4 c. brown sugar, packed
2 tsps. of all-purpose flour
1 tsp. lemon juice
1/2 tsp. cinnamon
1 - 9" unbaked pie shell

Combine apples with sugar, flour, lemon juice and cinnamon in medium bowl; pour into pie shell. Then combine eggs, pumpkin, evaporated milk, sugar, butter, cinnamon, salt and nutmeg in medium bowl and pour over apple mixture. Bake at 375° for 1 hour, or until a toothpick inserted in the center comes out clean.

Pumpkin Chiffon Pie

1 lg. can pumpkin
4 eggs, separated
1 c. light cream
1 c. brown sugar
1/2 c. coconut flakes
1-1/2 c. rum
2 envelopes unflavored gelatin
1 tsp. ea. cinnamon and ground ginger
1/2 tsp. ground nutmeg
1/2 tsp. ground allspice
salt.
1 9" unbaked pie shell

Bake pie shell for approx. 20 min. at 350° or until a nice golden brown.

Combine brown sugar, gelatin and spices in saucepan. Add cream, egg yolks and pumpkin, cooking over low heat 10 minutes or until mixture bubbles and gelatin is dissolved. Cool and add rum. Chill in the refrigerator for four hours. Beat egg whites until stiff and fold in sugar slowly. Fold egg whites into pumpkin mixture. Spoon onto the baked pie shell. Chill until firm, about 2 hours. Toast the coconut flakes on a baking sheet in a preheated 350° oven for 7 minutes or until lightly browned and sprinkle over pie. You can also add dollops of whipped cream on top of each serving.

Healthy Chiffon Pie

1 lg. can pumpkin
3 eggs, separated
1/2 c. light cream, hot
1/4 c. sweet cider
3 tbsps. molasses
2 tbsps. nutritional yeast
1 tsp. cinnamon
1/2 tsp. ea. ground nutmeg, ginger, cloves, allspice
1 9" baked pie shell (bake at 350° for approx. 20 min. or until golden brown)

Soften gelatin in cider. Dissolve in hot milk in top of double boiler with hot water in the bottom. Add pumpkin, molasses, spices, salt and yeast. Cook in double boiler until thick. Remove from heat. Cool to lukewarm. Beat in egg yolks. Cool. When mixture begins to set, beat with rotary beater. Beat egg whites separately until they are stiff, then fold then into the pumpkin-gelatin mixture. Pour into baked pie shell and chill until firm.

Pumpkin-Peanut Pie

1 lg. can pumpkin
1 c. chunky style peanut butter
3 egg yolks, beaten
1/2 c. light cream
1 c. heavy cream, stiffly beaten
3 egg whites, well beaten until stiff
1/2 c. brown sugar, packed
1 envelope plain gelatin
1/4 c. cold water
2 tsp. pumpkin pie spice
salt
1 - 9" pie shell, baked

Using a spatula, gently line sides and bottom of the 9" pie shell with 1 c. chunky peanut butter and set aside. Soften 1 envelope plain gelatin and 1/4 c. cold water and set aside. Blend pumpkin, sugar, cream, beaten egg yolks and spices, and cook over med. heat 5 minutes. Add softened gelatin and cook 5 minutes more. Cool. Beat the egg whites into the well-cooled pumpkin filling. Pour mixture into peanut butter lined piecrust and shill until set. At serving time, garnish with whipped cream.

Maple Pumpkin Pie

1 lg. can pumpkin
2 eggs
1 c. evaporated milk
3/4 c. maple syrup
2 tbsps. Sugar
2 tbsps. pumpkin pie spice
salt
1 nine-inch unbaked pie shell

Beat eggs well, then beat in sugar, spices and salt. Add maple syrup, evaporated milk and pumpkin, beating all with a mixer. Pour into the pie shell and bake in a 450° oven for 10 minutes, then reduce to 350° and bake 40 minutes longer - or until a knife blade comes out clean when inserted near center. This is very good served cold or slightly warm with natural Cheddar cheese.

Pumpkin Cheese Pie

1 lg. can pumpkin
1 lb. cottage cheese
2/3 c. brown sugar, firmly packed
2 eggs, beaten
1/2 c. butter
2 tbsps. brandy
2 tsps. pumpkin pie spice
1 - 9" pie shell, unbaked

Preheat oven to 450°. Put cottage cheese into blender and mix until it is smooth. In a large bowl, combine all ingredients and pour into unbaked pie shell. Put into oven for 10 minutes, then reduce temperature to 325°. Bake for 45 minutes or until knife inserted in center comes out clean.

Pumpkin-Custard Praline Pie

2/3 c. finely ground pecans, packed
1/2 c. brown sugar, firmly packed
4 tbsps. softened butter
1 - 9" pie shell, unbaked

Mix the above ingredients well and press firmly into the bottom of the pie shell. Bake in a hot oven for 450° for 10 minutes and then allow to cool.

1 lg. can pumpkin
2 eggs, well beaten
1 c. light cream
2/3 c. brown sugar, firmly packed
1 tbsp. flour
1 tsp. cinnamon
1/2 tsp. ea. ground cloves, nutmeg, ginger, mace

Combine above ingredients, beating until smooth and creamy. Pour into pie shell. Bake in slow oven (325°) for 45 minutes, or until knife inserted in center comes out clean. This is good served with some whipped cream on each slice.

Pumpkin Pie with Ginger Crust

Crust

1-1/2 c. gingersnap crumbs
1/4 c. brown sugar
1/2 c. melted butter

Mix ingredients above thoroughly and reserve 3/4 of the mixture for topping and press the remainder of it into a 9" pie pan, forming a crust of even thickness. Chill the crust in the freezer while making the filling.

Filling

1 lg. can pureed pumpkin
1 c. heavy cream, whipped

1 c. brown sugar, packed
2 tsps. pumpkin pie spice
1/2 tsp. salt

Stir pumpkin and other ingredients except the whipped cream and ginger crumbs mixture into a large pan over low heat for 4 - 5 minutes over medium heat, stirring constantly. Remove from heat and cool thoroughly. When pumpkin mixture is cool, fold in whipped cream. Fill the chilled crust with the mixture and sprinkle the reserved crumbs on top. Cover with foil and freeze. Thaw the pie at room temperature for a couple of hours, or you can serve it frozen.

Sour Cream Pumpkin Pie

1 lg. can pumpkin
3 eggs, separated
1-1/2 c. sour cream
1 c. whipped cream
1 c. brown sugar
1 tsp. cinnamon
1/2 tsp. ea. nutmeg, ginger, ground cloves
1 - 9" pie shell, baked

Heat 1 c. of the sour cream in a double boiler and then temporarily remove from heat. Mix the remaining 1/2 c. of sour cream with the pumpkin, sugar and spices. Beat egg yolks and add to the hot sour cream mix over the double boiler, stirring constantly until it has thickened, approx. 15 minutes. Remove from the fire and cool. Meanwhile, beat the egg whites until stiff and fold into the cooled pumpkin mixture. Fold in the whipped cream. Pour the mixture into the piecrust and bake at 325° for approx. 45 minutes, or until knife comes out clean.

Orange Pumpkin Pie

1 lg. can pumpkin
1 c. evaporated milk, scalded
2 eggs, beaten well
1/4 c. orange juice
2/3 c. brown sugar, packed
1 tsp. ea. cinnamon, nutmeg and ginger
1/2 tsp. ground cloves
1/4 c. boiling water
1/2 tsp. salt
1 9" pie shell, unbaked

Make a smooth paste of the spices and water. Add with the sugar, salt and beaten eggs to the pumpkin. Stir to blend thoroughly, then add hot milk. Stir in orange juice and pour immediately into the unbaked pie shell. Bake at 350° until pie filling is set and knife inserted in center comes out clean.

Tipsy Pumpkin Pie

In a large bowl, combine:
1/2 c. milk
1/2 c. heavy cream
3/4 c. brown sugar, packed
1 tsp. cinnamon
1/2 tsp. ea. ginger, nutmeg, ground cloves, allspice

Stir in:
1 lg. can pumpkin
3 well beaten eggs
1/4 c. applejack (or you can use a good rum or different brandy if you prefer)
1 - 9" unbaked pie shell

Pour well-mixed ingredients into the pie shell and bake in a preheated 350° oven for 50 or 60 minutes or until a knife inserted into center comes out clean. Serve with a dollop of whipped cream on each piece.

Pumpkin Pie the Old Way

1 small pie pumpkin, cut into sections with seeds, strings and skin removed
2 cups thinly sliced pumpkin pieces
2/3 c. brown sugar
1 well beaten egg
1 tbsp. flour
1 tbsp. vinegar
2 tbsps. corn syrup
1 tsp. cinnamon
1/2 tsp. ea. ginger, nutmeg, ground cloves, mace
1 - 9" pie shell, unbaked
9" pie crust top, also unbaked (I like to use the refrigerated crusts that are ready to use and come two to a package. I find them easily in the grocery stores.)

Combine all ingredients and fill the bottom pie shell. Place the top crust over and seal it around the edges, making some air holes in the center with a knife or fork. Take in a preheated oven at 450° on a cookie tray for 10 minutes, then turn down to 375° and continue to bake for 35 minutes or until the pie crust is golden brown. This is particularly good served warm with cheese slices.

Pumpkin Chocolata Pie

1 lg. can pumpkin
2 eggs, well beaten
1 c. light cream
2/3 c. brown sugar
1/2 c. finely chopped pecans or walnuts
1 tsp. vanilla extract
1 tsp. cinnamon
1/2 tsp. ea. ginger, nutmeg, ground cloves, allspice
salt
1 - 9" pie shell, unbaked

Mix all the above ingredients, and stir in the chopped nuts last.

Pour mixture into the unbaked pie shell for 45 - 50 minutes at 350° or until knife inserted in center comes out clean. Cool pie and prepare chocolata mixture below.

Melt in saucepan 2 oz. sweet chocolate. Add the following ingredients:
2 c. milk
1-1/2 tbsps. cornstarch dissolved in 2 tbsps. water
1/2 tsp. salt
2 tbsps. melted butter
1 tsp. vanilla

Stir well until this is smooth and seems spreadable. Then spread over pie. Chill and then serve with dollops of whipped cream on each piece.

Pumpkin Pineapple Pie

1 lg. can pumpkin
1 lg. can crushed pineapple, drained
2 eggs, well beaten
1 c. light cream
2/3 c. brown sugar
1 tsp. vanilla
1 tsp. cinnamon
1 tsp. ground ginger
1/2 tbsp. ground cloves, nutmeg, allspice
1 - 9" unbaked pie shell

Combine all ingredients and fill the pie shell. Bake in a preheated 375° oven for 45 - 50 minutes, or until a knife inserted in the center comes out clean. You can add 1/2 c. slivered coconut and some thin sliced Macadamia nuts for an interesting change.

Pumpkin Cranberry Cheese Pie

Pumpkin filling

1 lg. can pumpkin
1 sm. jar or 1 c. applesauce
1/2 c. light cream
2 eggs, well beaten
1/2 c. cheddar cheese, grated
2 tsps. pumpkin pie spice
1/2 tsp. salt

Cranberry filling

1 sm. can cranberry relish (You can substitute whole cranberry sauce if desired)
2 tbsps. orange juice
1 tbsp. cornstarch

1 tsp. orange zest
1 - 9" unbaked pie shell

Mix ingredients for cranberry filling and pour into pie shell. Mix pumpkin pie ingredients and pour over the top of the cranberry filling. Bake in preheated 375° oven for 45 - 50 minutes or until knife inserted in center comes out clean.

Pumpkin Alaskan Pie

1 lg. can pumpkin
3 egg yolks, beaten (egg whites will be used in meringue)
1-1/2 c. heavy cream
2/3 c. brown sugar
1/2 c. finely chopped walnuts
1/4 c. dark rum
l tsp. cornstarch
1/2 tsp. salt
1/3 c. finely chopped preserved gingerroot
1-1/2 tsp. pumpkin pie spice
2 tsps. grated lemon rind
1 - 9" pie shell, baked at 350° until golden brown

Meringue

3 egg whites
1/4 tsp. cream of tartar
1/2 c. sugar mixed with 1 tsp. vanilla

Scald cream and set aside. Beat egg yolks, stir in brown sugar and cornstarch, then add hot cream. Cook in double boiler until custard begins to thicken (about 180°), adding the salt. Remove from heat and mix pumpkin with ginger, pumpkin pie spice, and lemon rind, then stir into custard.

Fill bowl with ice and beat the mixture in a bowl over the ice while adding rum. When mixture is cool, fold in whipped cream, chopped nuts and minced gingerroot. Freeze in a metal bowl in the freezer. Beat twice during the two first half-hour periods of freezing. When it is frozen to an ice cream consistency, remove and fill pie shell, allowing the mixture to soften if necessary, then return to freezer. Just before serving, beat the egg whites with cream of tartar until the mixture has a firm meringue consistency. Fold in the vanilla sugar mixture. Spread the meringue over the pie, making sure edges are neatly sealed. Put into preheated 450° oven and bake until meringue is browned. This just takes a few minutes, so keep your eyes on it and be prepared to get it out of the oven quickly. Serve immediately.

Pumpkin-Mincemeat Pie

1 lg. can pumpkin
1-1/3 c. mincemeat (use prepared - you can get it in jars at the grocery store)
2 eggs, separated
1 can evaporated milk
2/3 c. brown sugar
1/2 c. chopped walnuts
2 tbsps. butter
2 tsps. lemon juice
1 tsp. grated lemon rind
1/4 c. rum (optional)
1 tsp. cinnamon
1/2 tsp. ground ginger, nutmeg, cloves, and allspice
1 9" prepared pie crust

Spread mincemeat in the bottom of 9-inch piecrust. Beat eggs in bowl and set aside. Blend in brown sugar and spices. Combine milk, pumpkin, butter, lemon juice, lemon rind and rum if desired in a saucepan; heat to scalding. Stir into egg mixture. Add walnuts Pour carefully over mincemeat layer. Bake at 425° for 45 to 50 minutes or until custard is set.

Calabasas Pie (Mexican Pumpkin Pie)

1 lg. can pumpkin
1 c, evaporated milk
2 eggs
1 c. brown sugar
Grated peel and juice of 1/2 lg. orange
1 tsp. cinnamon
1/2 tsp. ea. nutmeg and ginger
1/2 c. chopped pecans or walnuts
Whipped cream
1 9" prepared piecrust

Mix pumpkin, orange juice and sugar in saucepan and heat slowly. Turn mixture into blender and add spices, milk and eggs, blending until smooth. Line piecrust with nuts on bottom. Turn into piecrust and bake at 375° until blade inserted in center comes out clean. Cool and serve with whipped cream.

Pumpkin Pie with Rum Sauce

1 lg. can pumpkin
3 eggs, slightly beaten
1-1/2 c. evaporated milk

1 c. brown sugar
3/4 c. chopped walnuts
1 tsp. ea. cinnamon and ginger
1/2 tsp. cloves
1 9" prepared piecrust

Combine all ingredients and turn into the piecrust. Bake at 425° for 15 min. and then turn heat down and bake at 375° for 45 min. or until blade inserted in center comes out clean. Set aside to cool.

Rum Sauce

2 c. milk
4 egg yolks
1 c. sugar
1/2 c. rum
1/2 tsp. vanilla

Bring milk to a boil and stir in sugar. Bring to a boil again and continue to simmer for 15 min., stirring frequently. Remove from heat, add vanilla and cool. Beat egg yolks well. Gradually add a little of the cooled milk mixture to the egg yolks, then beat in the remainder of the egg yolks. Bring to a boil once more and remove from heat. Beat the rum into the mixture gradually. Pour into a jar and refrigerate until ready to serve with pieces of pie.

Heavenly Pumpkin Pie

1 can pureed pumpkin
1 c. evaporated milk
2 eggs, slightly beaten

1/2 c. brown sugar, packed
1 tsp. allspice
1/2 tsp. ginger, cloves, nutmeg
Mix all ingredients and stir until smooth. Set aside.

Cream Cheese Layer

1 pkg. cream cheese
1 egg, beaten
1/2 c. brown sugar
1/2 c. coconut
1 tsp. vanilla
1 9" prepared piecrust

Blend softened cream cheese, sugar and vanilla. Add beaten egg and mix well. Stir in coconut and spread into piecrust. Pour pumpkin mixture over cream cheese mix in piecrust. Bake at 375° for 1 hour or until knife inserted in center comes out clean.

Pie for the Health of It with Lemon Sauce

Piecrust

1 c. unbleached flour
1/2 c. flaxseed flour
1/2 c. softened butter
1-1/2 tbsps. cold water
1-1/2 tbsps. lemon juice

Cut butter into flour in a medium size bowl. Add water and lemon juice and mix well. Form into two balls of equal size. Roll out the balls on floured board for two piecrusts.

Filling

2 c. peeled and cubed steamed fresh pumpkin
3 eggs, beaten slightly
1 c. light cream
2/3 maple syrup
1 c. seedless raisins
2 tsps. pumpkin pie spice

Place pumpkin, raisins and syrup into blender, blending until smooth. In a large bowl, mix the remaining ingredients. Add the pumpkin mixture and turn into the unbaked piecrusts. Bake at 375° for 1 hour or until knife inserted in center comes out clean. Serve with Lemon Sauce below.

Lemon Sauce

3 tbsps. lemon juice
3/4 c. light cream
4 tbsps. honey
1 tsp. vanilla
1 tsp. grated lemon rind

Place all ingredients into blender and blend thoroughly. Pour into small pitcher and place in refrigerator to chill until ready to serve with pie.

Pumpkin Chocolate Cheesecake

Crust

3 c. crushed gingersnaps
1 c. butter, melted

Preheat oven to 350°. Oil 2 9" pie pans. Mix gingersnap crumbs and melted butter and press into the bottom of the pans equally. Bake 15 minutes, remove from the oven and set aside.

Filling

1 lg. can pumpkin
2 sm. cans sweetened condensed milk
6 eggs, separated
1 lg. package cream cheese, softened
1 c. sour cream
1/4 c. brown sugar
1 tsp. cinnamon
1/2 tsp. ea. ginger, nutmeg, allspice
2 oz. dark chocolate (you can use light chocolate if you prefer)
1/4 c. chopped pecans

Beat egg yolks until thick and lemon colored. Add softened cream cheese, beating until very smooth. Add pumpkin, condensed milk, and spices, beating again until well blended. In a separate bowl, beat egg whites until stiff and fold into pumpkin mixture. Just before pouring into piecrusts, melt chocolate in small pan, watching carefully. Stir melted chocolate into pumpkin mixture, allowing it to swirl in a marble pattern. Pour into pie shell and bake at 375° for 1 hour or until knife inserted in center comes out clean. Remove from oven and increase oven temperature to 450°.

Meanwhile, combine brown sugar with sour cream and spread on top of filling, then sprinkle with nuts. Return to oven and bake for 5 minutes. Remove from oven, cool and refrigerate until serving time.

Pumpkin Cheesecake

Piecrust

1 c. gingersnap crumbs
1/2 c. butter, melted

Mix gingersnap crumbs and melted butter in a small bowl and spread over the bottom of a 9" pie pan. Reserve a small amount of the crumb mixture for the topping.

Filling

1 lg. can pumpkin
1 lg. pkg. vanilla pudding mixture
2 c. light cream
1 lg. package whipped cream cheese
1/2 c. brown sugar, packed
2 tbsps. lemon juice
1 tsp. pumpkin pie spice
2 eggs, separated
2 envelopes unflavored gelatin

Mix pudding package and gelatin in a medium saucepan. Beat egg yolks and blend in light cream; stir into pudding mixture. Cook slowly, stirring constantly until mixture bubbles around edges. Slowly beat hot mixture into cream cheese in a large bowl. Stir in the pumpkin and lemon juice. Chill until mixture is somewhat firm. Meanwhile, beat egg whites until stiff, slowly beat in sugar. Then fold in meringue and whipped cream. Pour into piecrust and sprinkle remaining crumbs. Chill until firm.

Pumpkin and Apple Pie, Version 2

3 c. cubed, pared pumpkin
4 apples, peeled, cored and sliced thin
3 eggs, lightly beaten
1 c. sugar
1/4 c. seedless raisins
1/2 c. sauterne or other sweet white wine
1 tsp. fresh minced parsley
1/2 tsp. ea. rosemary, thyme, marjoram
salt and pepper
2 prepared piecrusts for a two-crust pie

Preheat oven to 450°. Sauté pumpkin cubes in butter in a large skillet until pumpkin is tender enough to mash. Put pumpkin in a large mixing bowl. Add cinnamon, wine, sugar and mix thoroughly. Blend in lightly beaten eggs. Add herbs, salt and pepper (as always, to suit your own taste) and mix well. Stir in apple slices and raisins.

Line a 9" pie pan with half the pastry dough. Pour in the filling. Put on the top portion of pastry dough and seal, fluting the edges and puncturing the top in several places to allow the steam to escape. Bake for 15 minutes and reduce heat to 375°. Continue to bake for 45 minutes or until knife inserted in center comes out clean. Remove from oven and allow to cool before serving.

CAKES

Easy Pumpkin Cake

1 c. canned pumpkin
1 pkg. yellow cake mix
1 c. oil
2 eggs
1 c. brown sugar
1/3 c. water
1 tsp. cinnamon
1 tsp. allspice
1/2 tsp. ea. Ginger, nutmeg and cloves

Prepare cake mix according to label directions but use the pumpkin and 1/3 c. water to replace regular liquid content of the cake. Beat in the eggs and seasonings.

Pour batter into a well-greased and floured 13 x 9 x 2" pan. Bake 30 - 40 min. at 350° or until cake is golden brown and top springs back when touched. Cook 5 min. on wire rack. Remove from pan and continue to cool.

Frosting for Easy Pumpkin Cake

(You can use a commercial frosting if you like and add 2 tbsps. orange juice and 1 tsp. grated orange rind)

3 c. sifted confectioners' sugar
boiling water
2 tbsps. orange juice
1 tsp. grated orange rind

If you are making the second version of the frosting, blend confectioners' sugar with 1 tbsp. orange juice, orange rind, and enough boiling water to give frosting a soft, but not runny consistency. Cut cake into 2" squares and dip tops into frosting.

Pumpkin Cake with Cream Cheese Frosting

1 lg. can pumpkin
3 c. flour
4 eggs, slightly beaten
1-1/2 c. brown sugar
1-1/2 c. oil
2 tsps. baking powder
2 tsps. baking soda
salt
1-1/2 tsp. pumpkin pie spice

Blend dry ingredients, add oil and mix until well blended. Add slightly beaten eggs and blend 1 minute longer. Do not over-mix.

Turn batter into 3 - 9" oiled pans. Bake at 350° for 40 minutes or until cake springs back lightly when touched in the center. Cool on a rack, then turn out and cool completely before frosting.

Cream Cheese Frosting

1 8 oz. pkg. cream cheese
1 box powdered sugar
1/2 c. butter
1/2 c. chopped raisins (candied fruit may also be added)

Combine sugar, cream cheese, vanilla and butter, stirring until you have a smooth mixture. Add raisins and frost. You can use the candied fruits as a garnish. Refrigerate until ready to serve.

Pumpkin Gingerbread

1 lg. can pumpkin
1 teaspoon ground cloves
1 c. all-purpose flour
1 c. whole wheat flour
2 lg. eggs
1 egg white, whipped with 1 tsp. plain sugar until stiff
1/2 c. molasses
2/3 c. brown sugar
1/4 c. vegetable oil
1/2 c. buttermilk
1 tsp. vanilla
2 tsps. ground ginger
1 tsp. cinnamon
1/2 tsp. nutmeg
2 tsps. baking soda
1/2 tsp. baking powder
salt

Preheat oven to 350°. Oil a 9-inch square baking pan. Combine dried ingredients in a large bowl. Combine remaining ingredients (except egg white). Fold pumpkin mixture into dry ingredients until well combined. Fold in egg white. Pour into prepared pan and bake 35-40 minutes wooden pick inserted in center comes out clean. Remove from rack and cool, or serve warm with whipped cream.

Lemon Frosted Pumpkin Cake

1 lg. can pumpkin
2 c. all-purpose flour
2 eggs
1/4 lb. butte
2 tsp. lemon extract
1 c. brown sugar
1 tsp. baking powder
1/2 tsp. baking soda
1 tsp. pumpkin pie spice
1 tsp. ginger

Preheat oven to 350°. Oil 9" square cake pan. Blend butter and sugar. Add eggs and extract and beat until smooth. Add pumpkin. In a separate bowl, mix all dry ingredients and add to pumpkin mixture, mixing until thoroughly blended. Pour batter into prepared pan and bake for 45 - 50 minutes or until toothpick inserted in center comes out clean.

Frosting

Juice and grated rind of 1 lemon
1/2 c. confectioner's sugar

Mix sugar, juice and rind and stir until sugar is dissolved. While cake is still warm, spoon frosting over cake top.

Pumpkin Blueberry Cake

1 lg. can pumpkin
4 eggs, beaten
3 c. flour
1 c. brown sugar

1 c. vegetable oil
2 tsp. baking powder
1/2 tsp. baking soda
1/2 tsp. salt
1 tsp. cinnamon
1/2 tsp. ea. nutmeg, ginger, cloves
1/2 c. pecans, chopped
3/4 c. blueberries

Preheat oven to 350°. Mix all dry ingredients together. Blend in eggs, pumpkin and oil, stirring until they are well blended. Mix in nuts and carefully fold in blueberries. Divide mix into 2 loaf pans and bake 45 - 50 min. or until knife inserted in center comes out clean.

Pumpkin Apple Cake

1 c. canned pumpkin
2 eggs
1-1/2 c. apples, finely chopped
1/2 c. chopped pecans
2-1/2 c. flour
1 c. brown sugar
1/2 c. butter
1 tsp. cinnamon
1/2 tsp. ea. nutmeg, ginger, cloves
1 tsp. baking power
1/2 tsp. baking soda

Preheat oven to 350°. Combine all dry ingredients including sugar. Then blend in butter and add eggs and pumpkin. Add apple and nuts, stirring in well. Pour into an oiled 13" cake pan and bake for 40 minutes, or until toothpick inserted in center comes out clean. Top with maple cream frosting.

Maple Cream Cheese Frosting for Pumpkin Apple Cake

10 ounces cream cheese at room temperature
5 tbsps. butter, room temperature
2 c. powdered sugar
1/4 c. + 2 tbsps. maple syrup

Beat cream cheese and butter in large bowl until light and fluffy. Add powdered sugar and beat at low speed until well blended.

Beat in maple syrup and chill 30 min. or until firm enough to spread.

Pumpkin Fruitcake

I can't help it; I am a fruitcake addict! I like the ones with real dried fruits and nuts in them and the ones where the fruit is soaked in rum and the cake is really most. You can only have the smallest slice because it is so rich, but for me, the winter holidays just aren't worth it if I don't have some fruitcake.

1 c. canned pumpkin
3-1/2 c. all-purpose flour
1 c. buttermilk
4 eggs
1 c. brown sugar
zest of one lemon and one orange
Juice of 1 lemon and 1 orange

Enough rum, mixed with juice of the lemon and orange, to cover the fruit.
1 c. pecans or walnuts (I like the whole halves, but you might want to chop yours up)
4 c. mixed dried fruit (dried apples, apricots, pineapple, cranberries, raisins, figs, dates or any combination you like)
1 tsp. baking powder
1/2 tsp. baking soda
1 tsp. ea. cinnamon, allspice, ginger
salt

Put all dried fruit into a bowl and cover it with a mixture of orange juice and rum. You need enough of the rum to cover the fruit. Soak for at least 24 hours.

Preheat oven to 350°. To make the cake, mix all dry ingredients, and then add the pumpkin, eggs, and buttermilk. When mixture is consistently blended, pour in the rum soaked fruits.

Bake about 60 minutes, or until knife inserted in center comes out clean. This cake can sit out, covered, and it will just keep getting better.

Candies

Pumpkin Coconut Candy

1 c. pumpkin
1 c. brown sugar
1 c. shredded cinnamon
1 tsp. cinnamon
1/2 tsp. ginger, nutmeg, cloves, allspice
1/2 c. finely chopped pecans

Combine all ingredients except pecans in saucepan over medium heat, stirring constantly until pumpkin mixture has a strong body like soft candy. Pour onto oiled flat plate or tin and cool. Shape into balls and roll the balls in the nuts. Chill before serving. You can also do this by pouring mixture into flat cake pan (9" is good), and then covering with the nuts and cutting into squares after chilling.

Pumpkin Nut Fudge

1/2 c. canned pumpkin
2 c. brown sugar, packed
1/2 c. heavy cream
3 tbsps. butter
1/2 tsp. walnuts, chopped fine
1 tsp. vanilla
1 tsp. cornstarch
1 tsp. cinnamon
1/2 tsp. nutmeg, allspice, ginger, cloves

Combine heavy cream, sugar and cornstarch in a saucepan over low heat until it simmers. Continue to simmer, stirring constantly, until a soft ball forms when the mixture id dropped into a small container of cold water. Remove from heat and add butter, pumpkin, spices and beat well. Add vanilla and nuts and stir until smooth. Spoon into an oiled 9" cake pan and cool. When fudge is cool, cut into squares and serve.

Mexican Pumpkin Candy

1 qt. fresh pumpkin, cubed and peeled (a small pumpkin should give you enough)
2-1/2 c. water
1 c. brown sugar, packed
1 c. raw sugar
1-1/2 tsp. pumpkin pie spice

Place the pumpkin in a saucepan, cover with the water, and bring to a boil. Reduce heat and simmer 15 - 20 minutes, or until pumpkin is tender but not mushy.

Remove pumpkin with a slotted spoon and place in bowl. Measure water left and there should be at least 1-1/2 c. water remaining. If not, add a little to make that amount. Add the sugar and the spice, and bring to a boil. Reduce head and simmer 15 min. Pour this mixture over the pumpkin pieces and allow them to stand overnight.

The next day, bring the pumpkin pieces in the sugar water mix to a boil, and then simmer 5 minutes. Remove the pieces with a slotted spoon again and then set them on a rack so they are not touching. Dry in a warm place or in the oven at 140° for 3 - 4 hours. Roll each piece in the raw sugar and set on waxed paper. You can store the pieces in a canister with layers separated by wax paper.

Pumpkin Peanut Spice Popcorn

1 bag microwave popcorn
1/2 c. shelled, salted peanuts
1 c. brown sugar
1 c. light corn syrup
3 tbsps.. butter
2 tsps. pumpkin pie spice
1 tsp. vanilla

Prepare popcorn according to instructions on package in microwave. Mix all ingredients except popcorn and peanuts in a heavy saucepan. Bring to a boil, then turn heat off. Pour all popcorn and peanuts into the spice mixture and mix until everything is coated. Allow mixture to cool and then break into chunks for serving.

Sweet Pumpkin Seed Trail Mix

1 c. hulled unroasted pumpkin seeds
1 c. pecans, coarsely chopped
1 c. hulled salted peanuts
1/2 c. coconut
1/2 c. brown sugar
1/4 c. butter

Melt butter in saucepan and add brown sugar. Remove from heat and add all seeds, nuts and coconuts, stirring until mixed well.

Pumpkin Butterscotch Fudge Bars

Preheat oven to 350°. Oil a large rectangular cake pan, 9" x 12".or the closest size to that.

1 c. all-purpose flour
1 c. quick oats
3/4 c. firmly packed brown sugar
1/2 cup chopped pecans
1/2 cup grated coconut
1/2 tsp. baking powder
1 tsp. cinnamon
1/2 tsp. ea. nutmeg, ginger, allspice, ground cloves
3/4 cup butter, melted

Combine all dry ingredients and mix in butter. Spread in pan Bake 15 minutes or until slightly brown. Cool in pan on wire rack.

Pumpkin Fudge

1/2 c. canned pumpkin
2/3 c. evaporated milk
1/2 c. brown sugar, packed
2 tbsps. butter
1 tsp. cinnamon
1/2 tsp. ea. nutmeg, ginger, allspice, ground cloves
1-1/2 c. butterscotch chips
1/2 cup pecans, chopped coarsely
1 tsp. vanilla

Combine all ingredients except chips, pecans and vanilla in a heavy saucepan. Bring to a boil and continue to boil for 8 - 10 minutes, or until somewhat thickened, stirring constantly. Remove from heat. Stir in remaining ingredients and pour over cookie base. Refrigerate until firm before cutting into bars.

APPENDIX

History

1. Betty Watson, *Cooks, Gluttons & Gourmets: A History of Cooking*, (Doubleday & Co. Inc., Garden City, NY), 1962
2. K.C. Chang, Editor, *Food in Chinese Culture: Anthropological Perspectives*, (Yale University Press, New Haven & London), 1977
3. Louise Andrews Kent, *The Vermont Year Round Cookbook*, (Houghton Mufflin Company, Boston), 1965
4. Louise P. DeGouy, *The Gold Cookbook*, (Galahad Books, NY), 1948
5. Don & Patricia Brodwell, *Food in Antiquity: A Survey of the Diets of Early Peoples*, (Frederick A. Praeger, NY), 1969
6. Louise P. DeGouy, *The Gold Cookbook*, (Galahad Books, NY), 1948
7. Hastings, Beck, *Meet the Cape Food*, (Purnell & Sons, Cape Town, South Africa), 1956
8. Gertrude I. Thomas, *Foods of Our Forefathers*, (F.A. Davis Co., Philadelphia), 1941
9. Waverly Root & Richard de Rochemont, *Eating in America: A History*, (William Morrow & Company, Inc., NY), 1976
10. U.P. Hedrick, *A History of Horticulture in America in 1860*, (Oxford University Press, NY), 1950
11. Ibid.
12. Ibid.
13. Reay Tannahill, *Food in History*, (Stein & Day, Publishers, NY), 1973

14. Gertrude I. Thomas, *Foods of Our Forefathers*, (F.A. Davis Co., Philadelphia), 1941

15. U.P. Hendrick, *A History of Horticulture in America to 1860*, (Oxford University Press, NY), 1950

Folklore

1. W. A. Clouston, *The Book of Noodles*, (A.C. Armstrong & Sons, NY), 1968
2. Adapted from: David Crocket Graham, *Songs and Stories of the Ch'uan Miao*, (Washington Smithsonian Institute), 1954
3. B. A Bodkin, Editor, *A Treasure of American Folklore*, (Crown Publishers, NY), 1944
4. B. A Bodkin, Editor, *A Treasure of New England Folklore*, (Crown Publishers, NY), 1947, 1965. Revised Edition
5. Ibid.
6. Ibid.
7. Maymie R. Krythe, *All About American Holidays*, (Harper & Brothers, NY, 1962

The Pumpkin and Its Relatives

1. Raymond Sokolov, "The Pumpkin Papers," (Natural History), October 1976
2. Barbara Friedlander, *The Secrets of the Seed: Vegetables, Fruits and Nuts*, (Grosset & Dunlap, NY), 1974

Growing Your Pumpkin

1. Barbara Friedlander, *The Secrets of the Seed: Vegetables, Fruits and Nuts*, (Grosset & Dunlap, NY), 1974
2. Hugh Wilbert, *Backyard Vegetable Gardening*,

(Galahad Books, NY), 1971
3. Ibid.
4. Ibid.

Pumpkins for Nutrition and Health

1. Betty Watson, *Cooks, Gluttons & Gourmets: A History of Cooking*, (Doubleday & Co. Inc., Garden City, NY), 1962
2. Barbara Friedlander, *The Secrets of the Seed: Vegetables, Fruits and Nuts*, (Grosset & Dunlap, NY), 1974
3. Ibid.
4. Ibid.

Storage and Preparation

1. Victor A. Tiedjens, *The Vegetable Encyclopedia and Gardener's Guide*, (The New Home Library, NY), 1943
2. Ibid.
3. Ibid.
4. Anne Moyer, Editor, *The Green Thumb Cookbook*, (Rodale Press Inc.), 1977
5. Ibid.
6. Ibid.
7. Ibid.

Sauces

1. Betty Watson, *Cooks, Gluttons & Gourmets: A History of Cooking*, (Doubleday & Co. Inc., Garden City, NY), 1962

Sweet Things

1. Gertrude I. Thomas, *Foods of Our Forefathers,* (F.A. Davis Co., Philadelphia), 1941

RECIPE INDEX

Tummy Ticklers, 62

Pumpkin Trail Mix, 62
Sesame Salt, 62
Pumpkin Munchies, 63
Peppery Curry Pumpkin Snacks, 63
Curried Pumpkin Seeds, 64
Toasted Pumpkin Seeds, 64
Pumpkin Milkshake, 65
Pumpkin Seed Cooler, 65
Winter Health Tea, 65
Pumpkin Sandwich, 66
Pumpkin Sandwich with Dates, Raisins and Cream Cheese, 66
Pumpkin Sandwich with Peanut Butter and Cranberry Sauce, 67
Pumpkin Hummus, 67
Pumpkin Cheese Dip, 68
Fried Pumpkin Blossoms, 68

Soups & Salads, 70

Chicken or Turkey Stock for Soups, 70
Sunshine Soup, 70
Curried Pumpkin Soup, 71
Vegetable Soup with Pumpkin, 72
Country Pumpkin Soup, 72
Caldito Calabasas, 73
Middle Eastern Pumpkin Soup, 74
Burmese Soup, 75
Japanese Pumpkin Soup, 76

Golden Pumpkin Soup, 77
Old English Soup, 78
Jamaican Pumpkin Soup, 79
Cold Pumpkin Soup With Almonds, 79
Cold Pumpkin Soup, Version II, 80
Pumpkin Soup With Gruyere Cheese, 81
Pumpkin-Apple Soup, 82
Yummy Pumpkin Soup, 82
Cream of Pumpkin Soup, 83
Pumpkin Soup Virginian, 84
Bean and Pumpkin Soup, 85
Chilled Pumpkin Soup with Grand Marnier, 85
Pumpkin and Oyster Soup, 86
Pumpkin Soup Grenada, 87
Spencer's Health Soup, 88
Bread and Pumpkin Soup, 88
Pumpkin Chestnut Soup, 89
Mexican Blossom Soup, 90
Pumpkin Soup with Black Beans, 90
Pumpkin Peanut Butter Soup, 91
Salad n' Seeds, 91
Autumn's Delights Salad, 92
Jellied Pumpkin Ring, 93
Apple-Pumpkin Salad, 93
Roast Pumpkin Salad, 94
Thai Pumpkin and Chicken Salad, 94
Pumpkin Coleslaw, 95
Pumpkin Dressing, 96

Breads, Batters & Biscuits, 97
Pumpkin Doughnuts, 97
Pumpkin Beignets, 98
Molettes de Calabasas (Pumpkin Muffins), 99
Pumpkin Pancakes, 99

Pumpkin Nut Waffles, 100
Pumpkin Sunrise Pancakes with Maple Cider Syrup, 101
Maple Cider Syrup, 101
Pumpkin Blossom Fritters, 101
Pumpkin Fritters, 102
Pumpkin Corn Fritters, 103
Pumpkin Apple Fritters, 103
Golden Harvest Biscuits, 105
Pumpkin Scones, 105
Egg glaze, 106
Pumpkin Dumplings with Hot Blueberry Compote, 106
Hot Blueberry Compote, 107
Pumpkin Hush Puppies, 108
Johnny Cakes, 108
Apple-Pumpkin Whole Wheat Muffins, 109
Pumpkin Raisin Nut Muffins, 110
Pumpkin Pineapple-Orange Nut Muffins, 110
Pumpkin Cornmeal Muffins, 111
Pumpkinseed Fruit Bars, 112
Pumpkinseed Crackers, 112
Rising Pumpkin Bread, 113
Land-of-Honey Pumpkin Bread, 113
Holiday Pumpkin Bread, 114
Jamaican Pumpkin Bread, 115
Pumpkin Peanut Bread, 115
Cactus Pear Pumpkin Bread, 116
Pumpkin Piñon Bread, 117
Pumpkin Chocolate Chip Bread, 117
Glaze Frosting, 118
Pumpkin Spice Muffins, 118
Hearty Pumpkin Banana Nut Muffins, 119
Pumpkin Sour Cream Muffins, 120
Streusel Topping, 120

Main Events, 121
American Stew in a Pumpkin, 121
Corn and Pumpkin Chowder in the Shell, 122
Pumpkin-stuffed Chicken, 123
Cajun Pumpkin, 123
Pumpkin Ranchero, 124
Pipian Empanadas, 125
    Dough, 126
    Filling, 126
    Hot Sauce, 127
Pumpkin Mole, 128
Pumpkin Mole II, 128
Stuffed Persian Delight, 129
Pumpkin Mexican Style, 130
Basque Pumpkin Stew, 131
Caribbean Pumpkin, 132
Mediterranean Stuffed Pumpkin, 133
African Pumpkin Stew, 134
Pumpkin and Cabbage Stew, 135
Pumpkin Chili, 135
Pork and Pumpkin Stew, 136
Pumpkin Tamales, 137
    Filling, 137
    Assembling and Cooking Tamales, 138
Prospector's Pumpkin, 140
Pig-in-a-Pumpkin, 141
Pumpkin Rarebit, 141
White Sauce, 141
Pumpkin-Cashew Cutlets, 142
Pumpkin Polenta, 143
Basic Polenta, 143
Pumpkin Lasagna, 144
Down Under Pumpkin Veggie Pie, 145

Pumpkin Ravioli, 145
Pumpkin Sauce for Raviolis, 147
Stuffed Pumpkin, 147

Asides, 149
Pumpkin with Cornmeal, 149
Pumpkin Blossoms Mediterranean, 149
Pumpkin Blossom Scramble, 150
Pumpkin Tips, 151
African Pumpkin Leaves with Peanuts, 151
Polish Sour Pumpkin, 152
Tacos al Flor de Calabasa (Pumpkin Blossom Tacos), 152
Pumpkin-Soy Bean Loaf, 153
Pumpkin Pudding Parmesan, 154
Incan Pumpkin, 155
Corn Meal Mush with Pumpkin, 155
Baked Pumpkin Patties, 156
    Sauce for Baked Pumpkin Patties, 156
Pumpkin in Coconut Milk, 157
Armenian Glazed Pumpkin, 157
Curried Pumpkin, 158
Pigs n' Pumpkin, 158
Pumpkin Omelet, 159
Pumpkin and Rice Casserole, 159
Pumpkin and Onion Casserole, 160
New England Baked Pumpkin, 160
Herbed Steamed Pumpkin, 161
Pumpkin Carrot Stew, 161
Deep-fried Pumpkin and Peanuts, 162
Green Pumpkin Stew, 163
Jeweled Pumpkin Ring, 163
Pumpkin Peel Tempura, 164
Pumpkin Roll, 165
Whole Pumpkin Tempura, 166

East Indian Pumpkin, 166
Pumpkin and Lentil Curry, 167
East Indian Gingered Pumpkin, 168
Pumpkin Baked in Cinnamon and Cream, 168
Corn and Pumpkin Stew, 169
Pumpkin Basque Style, 169

Sauces, 171
Pumpkin "Sause", 171
Pumpkinseed Mole, 171
Pumpkin Sauce for Chicken, 172
Pumpkin Raisin Seed Sauce, 173
Pumpkin Salsa, 173
Peanut-Pumpkin Sauce, 174
Pumpkin Sauce with Dates, 174
Pumpkin Pear Sauce, 175

Jams, Pickles, Drinks & Other Good Things, 176
Pumpkin Jam, 176
Old-Fashioned Pumpkin Marmalade, 176
Candied Pumpkin, 177
Pumpkin Conserve, 177
Pickled Pumpkin, 178
Pumpkin Flour, 178
Pumpkin Brew, 179
Pumpkin Shake, 179
Pumpkin Punch, 180
Pumpkin Soap, 181
Glycerin Pumpkin Soap, 182

SWEET THINGS

Puddings, 183
Pumpkin Bread Pudding, 183
Pumpkin Coconut Pudding, 184
Pumpkin Flan, 184
Pumpkin Rice Pudding, 185
Indian Pumpkin Pudding, 186
Pumpkin Coffee Mousse, 187
Pumpkin Custard, 187
Pumpkin Yogurt Custard, 188
Pumpkin Chocolate Pudding, 188
Plumpkin' Pudding, 189
    Hard Sauce for Pudding, 190

Cookies, 191
Pumpkin Peanut Butter Cookies, 191
Chunkin' Pumpkin Cookies, 192
Golden Pumpkin Health Cookies, 193
Pumpkin Pie Squares, 193
Pumpkin Sunflower Seed Bars, 194
Pumpkin Empanadas, 195
    Filling, 195
Pumpkin Poppy-Seed Cookies, 195
Pumpkin Chocolate Chip Cookies, 196
Pumpkin Bars, 197
    Pastry for Bars, 197
    Filling for Bars, 197

Piecrusts, 199
Basic Piecrust, 199
Oatmeal Piecrust, 200
Nut Piecrust, 201

Pies, 202
Dutch Pumpkin Pie, 202
Caramelized Pumpkin Pie, 202
All-American Pumpkin Pie, 203
    Extra for All-American Pumpkin Pie, 204
Pumpkin Pie with Butterscotch Sauce, 204
Butterscotch Sauce, 205
Pumpkin-Persimmon Pie, 206
Pumpkin Pye Recipe from *The Compleat Cook*, by W.M. London, 1655[1], 206
Pumpkin-Apple Pie, 207
    Pumpkin Layer, 207
    Apple Layer, 208
Pumpkin Chiffon Pie, 208
Healthy Chiffon Pie, 209
Pumpkin-Peanut Pie, 210
Maple Pumpkin Pie, 210
Pumpkin Cheese Pie, 211
Pumpkin-Custard Praline Pie, 211
Pumpkin Pie with Ginger Crust, 212
    Crust, 212
    Filling, 212
Sour Cream Pumpkin Pie, 213
Orange Pumpkin Pie, 214
Tipsy Pumpkin Pie, 214
Pumpkin Pie the Old Way, 215
Pumpkin Chocolata Pie, 216
Pumpkin Pineapple Pie, 217
Pumpkin Cranberry Cheese Pie, 217
    Pumpkin filling, 217
    Cranberry filling, 217
Pumpkin Alaskan Pie, 218
    Meringue, 218

Pumpkin-Mincemeat Pie, 219
Calabasas Pie (Mexican Pumpkin Pie), 220
Pumpkin Pie with Rum Sauce, 220
Rum Sauce, 221
Heavenly Pumpkin Pie, 221
    Cream Cheese Layer, 222
Pie for the Health of It with Lemon Sauce, 222
    Piecrust, 222
    Filling, 223
    Lemon Sauce, 223
Pumpkin Chocolate Cheesecake, 223
    Crust, 223
    Filling, 224
Pumpkin Cheesecake, 225
    Piecrust, 225
    Filling, 225
Pumpkin and Apple Pie, Version 2, 226

Cakes, 227

Easy Pumpkin Cake, 227
    Frosting for Easy Pumpkin Cake, 227
Pumpkin Cake with Cream Cheese Frosting, 228
    Cream Cheese Frosting, 228
Pumpkin Gingerbread, 229
Lemon Frosted Pumpkin Cake, 230
    Frosting, 230
Pumpkin Blueberry Cake, 230
Pumpkin Apple Cake, 231
    Maple Cream Cheese Frosting for Pumpkin Apple Cake, 232
Pumpkin Fruitcake, 232

Candies, 234

Pumpkin Coconut Candy, 234

Pumpkin Nut Fudge, 234
Mexican Pumpkin Candy, 235
Pumpkin Peanut Spice Popcorn, 236
Sweet Pumpkin Seed Trail Mix, 236
Pumpkin Butterscotch Fudge Bars, 237
Pumpkin Fudge, 237

ABOUT THE AUTHOR

I am a young-minded former senior mentor, advocate, and activist for physically, developmentally, and emotionally challenged children and adults.

Sometime in the late 60's, my younger and only sibling came home from Vietnam 100% disabled, and it gave me the heart to do this work, which I have continued to do for many years.

I am also an activist for anti-bullying of any age, belief system, or race of person. I pretty much say what I mean and mean what I say. My other book, filled with the writings of the lives of 23 physically challenged fiber artists is *Artful Alchemy: Physically Challenged Fiber Artists Creating.* I am also a fiber and mixed media artist. You can also read my blog: www.allinadayswork.wordpress.com.

I live with the love of my life, Richard Dean McCoy, our five Chihuahuas, a wayward cat, two huge goldfish and two alien catfish in Southern California.

Made in the USA
Columbia, SC
27 April 2022